See HOW Jesus Used Power!

See HOW Jesus Used Power!

Gerald H. Ihle

WINEPRESS WP PUBLISHING

Packaged by WinePress Publishing, PO Box 428, Enumclaw, WA 98022. The views expressed or implied in this work do not necessarily reflect those of WinePress Publishing. The author(s) is ultimately responsible for the design, content, and editorial accuracy of this work.

Unless otherwise noted, all Scriptures are taken from the Revised Standard Version of the Bible. Copyright 1946, 1952, 1971 by the Division of Christian Education of the National Council of the Churches of Christ in the U.S.A. Used by permission.

ISBN 1-57921-398-7
Library of Congress Catalog Card Number: 2001093242

ACKNOWLEDGMENTS

I would like to thank my supportive and helpful wife, Janet, for reviewing this manuscript line by line and for making suggestions that make for better readability.

I would also like to express my thanks to Mrs. Nancy J. Kessler for typing the manuscript in preparation for its publication; to Tammy Hopf, my project manager at Winepress Publishing, who guided me through the rigors of editing, finalizing the proofs, and answering my endless questions; and to my editor, Simeon Spillane, who smoothed out my rough edges and made many helpful suggestions to make for better readability.

Finally, I would like to express my gratitude to Rev. Dr. William W. Matz, Dean Emeritus of Moravian Theological Seminary and to Bishop Alfred Johnson, Resident Bishop of the New Jersey Episcopal Area of the United Methodist Church, who have so graciously endorsed my book.

CONTENTS

See How Jesus Used Power!

FOREWORD

In reading this new book in its manuscript draft, I am reminded of the intriguing words of an earlier hymn learned in my youth, "Tell me the story of Jesus, write on my heart every word. Tell me the story most precious, sweetest that ever was heard." There is something of that sentiment expressed in Pastor Ihle's new book, which engages and describes the simple but profound encounters of Jesus in physical and spiritual demonstrations illustrating aspects of power and applied faith. Power is displayed in a variety of vignettes involving miraculous results within people wrestling with perplexing circumstances while confronted with the ever existing but contrasting powers of good and evil.

A full array of Jesus' ministry comes into focus dealing with the forces of nature, healing, demon possession, raising from the dead, and the process of human transformation that results in the salvation of human beings in desperate circumstances. Jesus is portrayed as the source of power to God's people then and now—inside and outside the church.

See How Jesus Used Power!

This thoughtful treatment of the power of Jesus is a refreshing reminder of the story of Jesus and His giftedness in supplying life, faith, and power for the living of these days as we are receptive and ready to be made whole.

—Rev. Dr. William W. Matz, Dean Emeritus,
Moravian Theological Seminary,
Emeritus Vice-President,
Moravian College, Bethlehem, Pennsylvania
Adjunct Professor in Philosophy,
Northampton Community College, Bethlehem, Pennsylvania

Pastor Ihle unfolds for us an essential message of Jesus' purposes through His dramatic and revelatory use of power. He offers us a view of power usage as a means of grace to redeem and reconnect God's humanity with God as a way to draw all persons to Him.

He accurately reflects, reviews and assures us, through an abundance of Biblical witness, that Jesus, who has un-limited power, has chosen to use it to redeem, reconcile, and heal every broken and sinful condition of our human-ity, and shows us how this power for doing good can wholly address the nature of sin inextricably expressed in the per-sonal soul and in the social systems of injustice.

Through the Biblical story, Pastor Ihle reveals "how Jesus used power" to dispense power, engender the power in oth-ers, and, in fact, often insisted that we contribute our power of faith as a holy partner with Jesus in ours, and in the world's healing. But, above all, Jesus' witness to power ulti-mately points to the fact that all power belongs to an inex-haustibly loving and extravagantly gracious God.

This book is especially for you if you have experienced the bewilderment of "power failure," in Chapter 7, or if you have been an incurable "untouchable" but who has felt the liberating power to have been "touched" by Jesus in Chapter 10. Or again, you will appreciate the bottom line in Chapter 10, that "faith is power."

I commend this beautiful book of invitation to find power, experience power, and be offered the gift of power graced and given by Jesus, but even more, to accept the bold invitation to join Jesus in the joy of dispensing a power to create the Shalom of God in persons and in the world.

—Alfred Johnson, Resident Bishop
The New Jersey Episcopal Area
The United Methodist Church

PREFACE

There is a great power struggle going on in the world today, one that has been present throughout history. It is a power struggle between the forces of good and evil, between Satan and God. And while evil seems to be winning so much of the time, *The Bible* affirms that, at the last, good will triumph.

To this end, Jesus' followers have been praying for centuries the prayer that He taught His disciples to pray: "Thy Kingdom come, Thy will be done, on earth as it is in heaven" (Matthew 6:10-11). Some day that prayer will finally be answered and God's Kingdom will be here on earth.

In the meantime, there seems to be no end to the news of evil powers winning over the good, to killing and robbery, to injustice and corruption. Wars seem endless as people in power are often captive to greed and deceit. Mass millions experience oppression by the powerful. Terrorism by hateful people in the name of religion is alarmingly on the rise in today's world. Our nation mourns the loss of thousands of lives in the dreadful September 11, 2001 evil attack on the World Trade Center in New York City and the

Pentagon in Washington D.C. that brought our nation to the brink of war with fanatical fierce terrorists.

There is a longing in humanity for peace and justice, for truth and kindness, for integrity and love, for an end to hate and to the atrocities of war and crime, for an end to violence, and an end to indifference toward human suffering and starvation. Generation after generation, we long for healing and restoration. And it *will* come . . . in God's time.

The Bible confirms that the day *is* coming when good will finally triumph over evil . . . when the Messiah will return and Satan will be defeated once and for all. Death will not have the final say then—because there is life after the grave. Concerning this final victory of good over evil, Paul said it so well in his New Testament letter:

> Then comes the end, when He delivers the kingdom to God the Father after destroying every rule and every authority and power. For He must reign until He has put all enemies under His feet. The last enemy to be destroyed is death.
>
> —1 Corinthians 15:24–26

So ends the great power struggle of the ages between good and evil, Jesus and Satan, spirit and flesh. This book will endeavor to portray some of the ways Jesus used the immense power He was given by the Heavenly Father and to show how He shared that power with people of faith during His three-year earthly ministry. In it, the reader will be reminded that Jesus, by His own choice, refused to exercise power to benefit Himself, but always chose to use it for the benefit of others and for the glory of His Heavenly Father. We will see that there is much to gain from examining His perfect use of an awesome trust and resource: power.

The Nature of Power

Power can, of course, be used for good or for evil. Power can heal and restore, or power can destroy and kill. Power can build up or tear down. Our modern world (as certainly the ancient world did) has witnessed terrible abuses of the power which rests in evil hands. Power-hungry leaders have frequently seized control of society's power structures and brought great harm to the nations of the world.

The power to destroy millions is now available through modern weapons of mass destruction. Appallingly, technology now offers nuclear weapons that can be delivered by lethal missiles. Chemical and biological warfare are modern threats to world security. At the same time, modern technology offers power to benefit millions with revolutionary advances in medicine, agriculture, transportation, communications, science, education, and the mass media.

Never before in history have the opposing powers on earth—forces for good and for evil—been as great as they are in our present generation. And while these two powers have always been in confrontation with one another to bring blessings upon humanity with good—or to curse humanity with evil—their purposes have never been as divided.

Surely, power in the hands of evil, hateful, and ignorant people can cause immense harm. Likewise, power in the hands of good, moral, wise, and compassionate people can bring incredible benefit and blessing to humanity and to the environment. Power, as a force, then, is only as good or as evil as the will that directs it, and the end that its use is directed toward.

Weakness is the opposite of power. We would prefer weakness to be in evil hands and power to be in good hands. But, all too often, power ends up in the hands of evil people and good people end up wielding weakness. Jesus Christ, for example, was not weak, as some charged. In fact, He represented and carried within Himself enormous power, yet this was not *worldly* power. Christ had spiritual power. He was strong, but not in a military, economic, or ecclesiastical sense. Perhaps this is why His power was misunderstood by worldly men.

Jesus' power was a great threat to those contemporaries of His who *were* in political power. He was a King but, as He endeavored to explain to those who followed Him, His Kingdom was different than that of worldly kingdoms. Jesus tried to explain to Pontius Pilate what His Kingdom was all about: "My kingship is not of this world" (John 18:36).

Jesus made no apology about His access to power when He was made to appear before Caiaphas, the high priest of Jerusalem, and other religious leaders:

> But I tell you, hereafter you will see the Son of man seated at the right hand of power, and coming on the clouds of heaven.
>
> —Matthew 26:64

This claim of Christ enraged the high priest so much that he tore his priestly robes and charged Jesus with blasphemy. Why? Power such as Jesus was claiming was a definite threat to his own!

Still, Jesus only displayed *samples* of His true, limitless spiritual power at times. He offered samples of rebirth conversions, healing miracles, casting out demons, miraculous feedings of thousands of people, and even raising the dead.

Death itself could not claim Him for more than three days. After this, in His Resurrection, He was lifted up to heaven where no power on earth could touch Him. And He will return with ultimate power as ruling Messianic King and Judge . . . when every knee shall bow before Him! Power in Jesus Christ's control is power in good hands, in the best hands of all.

Conversely, the abuse of power is destructive and often violent. Jesus saw that power for good or evil rested with whomever was using or abusing it. He used the power He wielded wisely and unselfishly; modeling a nonviolent, compassionate use of power. He described the contrasting use of power this way:

> The thief comes only to steal and kill and destroy; I came that they may have life, and have it abundantly.
> —John 10:10

In his New Testament letter, James described how nations often use power to selfish, nationalistic, greed-motivated ends:

> What causes wars, and what causes fightings among you? Is it not your passions that are at war in your members? You desire and do not have; so you kill. And you covet and cannot obtain; so you fight and wage war.
> —James 4:1–2

Yet from the very beginning of His ministry, Jesus determined how He would use His God-given power. He rejected Satan's tempting offer to help Him build His Kingdom by using and abusing the powers of force and of the sword—the world's manner of empire-building. The kingdoms of this world were offered to Jesus by the "Prince of this world"—*if* Jesus would but honor and worship Satan instead of God (Luke 4:5–7). If only overzealous followers of Christ in later centuries had also scorned Satan's tempting offers to build the Kingdom by the sword! Countless lives could have been spared the ravages of the European religious wars and the bloody persecutions of Christians by Christians (including Roman Catholics and

Protestants alike) who happened to be in power at a given time or place.

The dreadful and cruel treatment of believers at the Inquisition and the treacheries of the Crusades are a blight on the Christian heritage. Protestants, Roman Catholics, Orthodox Christians, Jews, and Muslims alike all suffered atrocities for their particular religious persuasions by the unChristlike condemnations of powerful Christian leaders and their blind followers, who were all too eager to use the power of the state to kill dissenters, whom they regarded as guilty of heresy and treason. Satan drove many of Christ's leaders to a doctrinal hateful intolerance, forcing many Christians to flee their homes for refuge in other countries to secure religious freedom and access to biblical truth.

Somehow, many of Jesus' followers misinterpreted Jesus' teachings and example of love about how His Kingdom should grow and extend around the world. Yet Jesus refused to use power to force anyone to become a follower. He would use His power in other ways to advance His Kingdom on earth. His followers were intended to use power as the Lord directed—in compassionate, tolerant, and loving ways . . . to heal, not to destroy life. Jesus made it very clear how His true followers would be identified when He said:

> By this all men will know that you are my disciples, if you have love for one another.
> —John 13:35

Jesus gave no mandates to persecute anyone, nor directives to use State religion to kill anyone for heresy or for being a dissenter from the established religion of the majority. Jesus spoke about being persecuted, not about being a *persecutor* in the name of God:

. . . indeed, the hour is coming when whoever kills you will think he is offering service to God.

—John 16:2

Blessed are you when men revile you and persecute you and utter all kinds of evil against you falsely on my account.

—Matthew 5:11

Jesus never authorized the Church to use the sword of the state to enforce Christian discipleship. Instead, Jesus taught His followers to continue the use of His power for compassionate acts of healing and love for a lost world needing salvation. The cross is a reminder that Jesus suffered and died under state religion rather than seeking the defense of the sword. Jesus offered a cross to His followers, not a sword! There is more power in the cross than in the sword. The apostle Paul understood this well when He wrote to the Christians in the city of Corinth, Greece:

For the word of the cross is folly to those who are perishing, but to us who are being saved it is the power of God.

—1 Corinthians 1:18

Chapter One

HE COULD CALM A STORM

And He awoke and rebuked the wind, and said to the sea, "Peace! Be still!" And the wind ceased, and there was a great calm.

—Mark 4:39

The Sea of Galilee in Israel was one of Jesus' favorite places. He spent a lot of time in that area. It was the home of Peter and the other fishermen apostles, who lived at Capernaum on its northern shore.

After seeing this place for myself, I don't wonder why Jesus liked to be there! The Sea of Galilee is a beautiful lake, with mountains of the Golan Heights and Mount Hermon in the distance. The St. Peter's fish caught there still make for a memorable meal.

During His three-year ministry, Jesus would have crossed the lake by boat many times. In fact, he once preached to a crowd of people from a fishing boat by the shoreline. The lake is large, thirteen miles long, seven miles across and as deep as 130 to 157 feet in places. The south end empties into the Jordan River. Whether one views the beauty of the lake from a boat, from a hotel window, or walking along its shoreline, it is awesome to imagine Jesus coming here often. Indeed, because of its association with the "Lord of wind and waves," the lake seems like a holy place. Next to Jerusalem, the Sea of Galilee is my own favorite area of the Holy Land.

While majestically serene, a sudden storm can cause danger to small fishing boats out on the water. Indeed, this is what happened to Jesus and His disciples. They were crossing the lake when a violent storm suddenly arose and frightened even those experienced fishermen apostles, who had survived many a storm in the past. This particular storm was so bad that waves were filling the boat with water. The night was dark. And Jesus was sleeping through it all!

The apostles were alarmed and woke the Master. They seemed to feel that Jesus didn't care that they might all lose their lives in this storm. Indeed, they were so upset that they questioned Jesus, "Teacher, do you not care if we perish?" (Mark 4:38).

There seemed to be two storms that needed calming: the storm on the waters and the storm of fear in the hearts of Jesus' followers. Jesus needed to calm both storms to bring peace and stillness. But who could still storms at sea? Who had control over the wind and the rolling waves? Who could bring peace to the fearful hearts of veteran fishermen who knew danger when they saw it?

This was a big storm, and the men on board felt helpless. This would be a real test for Jesus. Jesus never used His power just for show. But, to *save* lives, this was different. Jesus spoke to the wind and sea: "Peace! Be still" (Mark 4:39).

That's it. It was Jesus' spoken word. His words calmed the whole situation. The wind died all down and the lake

was still. There they were under the night sky . . . in a boat
. . . on calm waters. Now that's power!

Next Jesus dealt with the other storm—the one within
His awed disciples, who before had been so frightened and
upset. Again, it was Jesus' spoken word that had power. He
said to them: "Why are you afraid? Have you no faith?"
(Mark 4:40).

With this simple question, our Lord calmed the men.
Apparently, He saw *faith* as the necessary resource they
seemed to have forgotten. As long as Jesus was in the boat
with them, weren't they safe? Faith, evidently, is supposed
to suppress fear. According to Jesus, faith is power. Was
this a lesson to be learned for the future? No doubt it was
never forgotten.

There is a psalm that affirms the power of faith over
fear within the storms of life:

> God is our refuge and strength, a very present help in
> trouble. Therefore we will not fear, though the earth
> should change, though the mountains shake in the heart
> of the sea; though its waters roar and foam, though the
> mountains tremble with its tumult.
>
> —Psalm 46:1–3

God speaks these words of comfort to His people who,
even today, are passing through the storms of life:

> Be still, and know that I am God. I am exalted among
> the nations, I am exalted in the earth! The Lord of hosts
> is with us, the God of Jacob is our refuge.
>
> —Psalm 46:10

And God *will* eventually still the noise of wars on the
earth. His Word says:

23

> The nations rage, the kingdoms totter; He utters His voice, the earth melts.
>
> —Psalm 46:6

Faith is power. God's Word is power. Jesus' words were power to still a storm. Yes, to witness someone stilling a storm would be as awesome to us as it was for the apostles:

> And they were filled with awe, and said to one another, "Who then is this, that even wind and water obey Him?"
>
> —Mark 4:41

Remarkably, we have the same opportunity to behold how Jesus calms the raging storm's of life with His words as His apostles did when He walked with them. We have the same need for faith in Him.

Walking on Water

There is another storm story in the Gospels. Once again, the disciples were out on the Sea of Galilee during a severe storm, with waves pounding against the sides of the boat. But this time Jesus was not in the boat with them. This time Jesus walked on the water toward the boat. The disciples were terrified when they saw someone walking on the water; thinking it must be a ghost. Then Jesus calmed their storm of fear with the words: "Take heart, it is I; have no fear" (Matthew 14:27).

Peter was so impressed with the display of such power, the power to walk on water, that He immediately wanted power to do the same thing. He asked Jesus for permission to walk toward Him on the water. Without hesitation, the Lord gave him permission, directing Peter to come to Him with the simple word, "Come."

Always the impetuous one, Peter climbed out of the boat, onto the water, and started to walk toward Jesus. But the wind was still blowing. Peter's initial act of faith soon shattered. Fear overcame his faith and down he went. Starting to sink, he cried out for help. That was a plea from a humbled believer!

It's always hard to say, "I need help." Peter had just done something none of the other apostles had *dared* to do. He had walked on water! But the wind scared him. Storms can do their work . . . even on people of faith. Could this be a lesson for us? Can we keep the faith, refuse to give up, even in the worst of storms? Then, as now, fear was the enemy, not the storm. Not the wind, not the waves, but the need for more faith in a very present Savior, with the power to calm a storm.

We Walk by Faith

The other apostles sat safely in the boat while Peter was exercising his faith. Peter at least had *tried*, even if he eventually went under. And Jesus did rescue the fisherman who dared to walk, if only for a moment, where others had feared to tread. Afterwards, Jesus coached Peter about this critical moment. He questioned Peter on why he had lost faith, saying, "O man of little faith, why did you doubt?" (Matthew 14:31).

Doubt itself was held up to question. Nevertheless, the man of "little faith" still had walked on water. If "little faith" can do that, does it not reveal something about faith's power? Peter and Jesus climbed back into the boat, and the wind stopped blowing. To witness such an awesome event evoked an awestruck response from the disciples, who proclaimed, "Truly, you are the Son of God" (Matthew 14:33).

Experiencing such power convinced Jesus' men, once again, that their Master was more than just a great teacher. He was God's Son. He had a direct power Source just waiting to be tapped, a supernatural power that could only come from God. And it was a power that Jesus wanted to share— if one were ready for it.

Peter was ready. But such power was difficult to maintain when fear got in the way. It wasn't the water or the wind that was the problem. It was fear and too little faith. It was doubting at the very moment when only faith would do. It was human weakness failing to keep itself strengthened by the power of faith—even when Christ was present!

Moreover, it was Jesus' ability to maintain faith without fear or doubt that enabled Him to do all that He did during the three ministry years before His Crucifixion. Healing, teaching the masses, raising people from the dead, and feeding multitudes, for example, were all acts of great faith. Perfect power, it would seem, can only be exercised in perfect faith.

Chapter Two

A Boy's Lunch Feeds Thousands

And those who ate were about five thousand men, besides women and children.

—Matthew 14:21

A headline reading "A Boy's Lunch Feeds Thousands" would certainly draw attention today. Such an event actually happened in Jesus' time! In fact, Jesus' feeding of thousands of people from a young boy's lunch of five loaves of bread and two fish is the only miracle that is recorded in all four Gospels. That miracle got everybody's attention!

The hunger of thousands of people needing food against the realistic resources of only five loaves of bread and two fish . . . that's not much provision to feed such a crowd. The need must have seemed overwhelming in human terms. Just so, problems today can seem so large that no one knows where to start in seeking to remedy them.

Today, hunger plagues millions. Famine, unemployment, and poverty deprive countless peoples worldwide of their daily bread. Crime threatens us everywhere. The threat of nuclear and chemical war casts a shadow on the earth. Natural disasters like earthquakes, tornados, and floods leave thousands homeless. Medical needs can quickly drain financial resources.

In all, the world's need can seem so great and over-whelming that one could easily despair over any possibility of helping others. As we hear the never-ending daily newscasts of tragedy and want, "compassion fatigue" has become a common experience. Still, if no one cared *what* happened in the world, no one would do anything—and we'd all just walk away. Thank God, there *are* people who do care about the suffering of others and who and try to do something about it.

Jesus cared about people. He wanted His followers to care, also. Caring, an expression of love, is a good place to start. Jesus started with love . . . then exercised His power in response to it. Power in the hands of loving and caring people can do a lot for needy people and make a difference on earth.

When Jesus performed this miracle, a crowd of five thousand people was gathered around Him. That's more than the normal church dinner crowd! Five hundred hungry people, even today, would put a strain on a local church food kitchen. Remarkably, the disciples' reaction to the large, hungry crowd late in the day was to advise Jesus to send them away to go buy supper somewhere else. Jesus countered their proposal with a directive to do the seemingly impossible. Jesus said, "You give them something to eat" (Mark 6:37).

Fulfilling that directive would require a lot of money to purchase food for the crowd, so how could the disciples do it? They quickly counted the food resources on hand, which added up to five loaves of bread and two fish, the donation of one lunch from a generous young boy in the crowd. These resources seemed like a joke for the large crowd out there.

It was enough for Jesus. With Him, a little would become a lot. Somehow, we don't know how, Jesus multiplied those meager resources over and over again so that five thousand people's stomachs were filled, leaving twelve baskets of food leftover for someone to take home, like leftovers from a covered dish church supper! This was an incredible display of power.

It is interesting that Jesus stood by His original directive for the disciples to feed the crowd, even in the midst of His miraculous act of provision. Yes, Jesus would supply the food miraculously, but He let the *disciples* be part of its distribution to the crowd. The scene created is a marvelous demonstration of God's power working in unison with people by faith.

Jesus directed that the crowd be split up into manageable groups of fifty persons each. Suddenly, the crowd looked smaller when it was divided into smaller groups. Now, as the Lord directed, the disciples would move out among one hundred groups and distribute food to each.

> And taking the five loaves and the two fish, He looked up to heaven, and blessed and broke them, and gave them to the disciples to set before the crowd. And all ate and were satisfied.
>
> —Luke 9:16–17

Apparently, in Jesus' mind, the disciples were not meant just to be spectators of this miracle. They would be key participants in the distribution of nourishment to others. They would be able to look out over individual faces of hungry people and offer them food. Now they were not just helpless bystanders. Jesus needed them for the serving.

They would take the food to the people. They were part of something great happening that day when a boy's lunch fed thousands.

Only John's gospel gives details on how the boy's lunch was found. John writes in his gospel that the apostle Andrew found the boy with the lunch, which he hadn't yet eaten. A child's donation was all Jesus used. I didn't say Jesus *needed* the boy's donation. I said Jesus *used* it. Why?

Jesus may have wanted to show how God can multiply little into much. He may have wanted to give the disciples something meaningful to do as well. The result was that five thousand people were filled. The overwhelming need was met by the Master with the cooperation of a young boy and twelve men we know as Christ's disciples.

Could this demonstration of power contain a lesson for us? Might a few people with a few resources, caring love, and faith become part of something similarly great in our needy world today? Can our Lord *still* multiply small, dedicated resources many times over? If that is so, perhaps modern Christians can dare to dream more largely of things that, with God's help and power, can be accomplished on earth.

Such organizations as Samaritan's Purse, World Vision, American Red Cross, and Salvation Army have inspired individuals to make donations, many of them small, that have made a tremendous impact on helping the hungry and homeless of the world.

As we start by caring, we may experience a new vision of the greater capabilities of the local church and the individual believer. We may see possibilities rather than obstacles to loving faith in action.

Chapter Three

TEAM MINISTRY FAITH

And behold, men were bringing on a bed a man who
was paralyzed, and they sought to bring him in and lay
him before Jesus; but finding no way to bring him in,
because of the crowd, they went up on the roof and let
him down with his bed through the tiles into the midst
before Jesus.

—Luke 5:18–19

The four Gospels tell one story from the viewpoint of
four different men who were followers of Jesus: Matthew, Mark, Luke and John. In all, they give an account of
a loving Savior who walked the earth, healing sick people
and bringing them to faith in God. Yet many crippled and
sick people couldn't get to Jesus on their own. They needed
others to bring them. People who brought others to Jesus
were part of a "team healing ministry." They became Jesus'
helpers:

Now when the sun was setting, all those who had any
that were sick with various diseases brought them to

Him; and He laid His hands on every one of them and
healed them.

—Luke 5:40

One such story in the Gospels is about four men of faith
who brought a paralyzed man to Jesus. They believed Jesus
had the power to restore their friend. It's good to have believing friends like that. They were determined to get the
paralyzed man before Jesus in spite of the obstacles. A crowd
had gathered to hear Jesus teach. But it would take more
than one man to carry the paralyzed man. It would take a
group effort, a team ministry.

In actuality, according to Luke's account, it took even
more than the physical effort of four men. Beyond "muscle,"
it took the faith of four men—who believed so much in
what Jesus was able to do that they would spare no effort in
getting their paralyzed friend to Him.

Actually, Luke's gospel doesn't tell us how *many* men
carried the man. That number comes from Mark's gospel
(Mark 2:3). But these four nameless men became heroes
through their persistent and creative rescue operation. How
did they do it?

First, they somehow had to get past the crowd. Many
times crowds get in the way of rescue workers and have to
be told to back away. It must have seemed an impossible
task to get their sick friend near enough to Jesus to receive
His healing touch with all the people surrounding Him.
Then someone had an idea. They would lift the man up on
the roof. Then they would remove some roof tiles and lower
the man down—right where Jesus was teaching! They
would interrupt Jesus right in the middle of what He was
saying. You can imagine the impression this made on the
Master. The Bible says, ". . . when He saw their faith . . ."
He immediately exercised His power (Luke 5:20). The

paralyzed man had consented to all this effort as well. Certainly, the same as his friends, he had to have been a believer in Jesus as well.

Jesus saw daring faith in those men that day. It took a lot of nerve to do what they did. Nobody scolded them. Instead, Jesus was impressed. But He did respond unexpectedly. Jesus did not immediately heal the man, as they were hoping. They had gone to all this effort to get physical healing of their friend's paralyzed body. But Jesus granted the man something even more valuable. He offered the man salvation, forgiveness of his sins, a spiritual healing. First things first. Would that be the reward for their faith? The Scripture says it this way:

> And when He saw their faith He said, "Man, your sins are forgiven you."
>
> —Luke 5:20

These words of assurance, words of pardon, were too much for some of the religious leaders of the day who heard Jesus say this to the man. Indeed, they viewed such pronouncements as heresy, arguing that only God had the authority to forgive sin. "Who is this that speaks blasphemies?" asked the scribes and Pharisees. "Who can forgive sins but God only?" (Luke 5:21).

Jesus must surely have realized what a problem such a declaration as ". . . your sins are forgiven you" might raise. Thus, He knew *exactly* what He would do and say next. Their questionings were just what He wanted. The critics had set themselves up for a miraculous response. Jesus would give them evidence of His authority and power to bring salvation and forgiveness.

First, He asked those who were judging Him a question "Which is easier, to say, 'Your sins are forgiven you,' or to say, 'rise and walk?' (Luke 5:23)" Jesus would next demonstrate that He had the authority to do both—to declare salvation and to order someone to rise up and walk—and that both times His words would become reality. The power of the Word, spoken by Jesus, would bring salvation and physical restoration to a paralyzed sinner.

Modern critics of the church might ask, "Is that all you're going to offer, salvation and forgiveness? Is that the *best* you can do?" Many might regard salvation as something of little value, and need of a Savior as negligible, not realizing the desperation of the human situation of sin and evil worldwide.

In countless churches across the land, Holy Communion is offered freely, yet countless people regard the sacrament of little worth, a non-essential for busy people who think they are doing the best they can and stand "in need of nothing" spiritually. Our Lord saw the sick man's spiritual need as primary, however. He addressed his need for forgiveness before physical health.

After Jesus pronounced salvation and was challenged by the Pharisees for so doing, He then spoke strong words to the paralyzed man, whom He had just granted salvation. These were powerful, directive words: "I say to you, rise, take up your bed and go home" (Luke 5:24).

Those few words, spoken by a powerful Christ, brought immediate results. To the surprise of everyone present, the man immediately got up, picked up his bed, and walked home—just as Jesus had told him to do. Jesus didn't tell him to stay around. He told him to go home, and he did. And the man did one more thing: He glorified God.

Imagine how the man's rescue team felt. It was an impressive sight. Their faith and efforts got results. Team ministry faith could now sit back and thank God they had all kept faith and not given up when the crowd got in the way. What if they had not kept faith in Jesus? Their friend would still be paralyzed and joyless, as well as guilt-ridden.

"Rise Up and Walk."

Even as this man was physically paralyzed, many today are crippled in other ways. Some are crippled emotionally, depressed—even suicidal. Some have deep emotional pain and scars from all types of physical and verbal abuse, or traumatic experiences in their past. Many are terribly discouraged and cope daily with debilitating low self-esteem. Bitterness and anger possess some to the point of being ready to do violence at the slightest provocation.

Others are crippled by addiction to drugs or alcohol. Fear paralyzes countless people. Racism, which has systematically poisoned our society, has crippled all too many through its lies and proud hatred. Many feel they are no good because parents, teachers, or peers have always told them they can't ever do anything right or that they have some physical defect. Still others have no motivation to work or achieve because no one has ever inspired them to greater heights of achievement. Who will bring those who suffer with these discomforts before Jesus?

When Christians pray for the sick, they need to remember to include not only the physically sick, but also the emotionally, mentally, and spiritually ill among us—who are in desperate need of salvation. Each church should remember to uphold the sick in their prayers. Prayer chains, prayers for the sick during worship, prayer retreats, prayer vigils, personal prayer, are all important in bringing people to Jesus for healing. Many simply need to bring people to church so that they are exposed to the healing touch of the powerful Christ who changes darkness into light and sadness into joy.

In every church there are older people, handicapped people, and emotionally disturbed people who need to be brought by someone to the healing place of church worship, where Christ is powerfully present. "Team ministry faith" remembers these people and finds some way to transport them to where faith in Christ is being taught and His Name honored.

Today's team ministries probably won't have the problem of getting past crowds in church with persons they are bringing to Jesus. Crowded churches are not a serious problem in American society today. Crowds *ought* to be a problem, but for the most part, they aren't. Sadly, many people don't get too excited over churches that prioritize salvation. Is salvation of so little worth to people? Does Jesus' death on a cross for the salvation of the world mean so little anymore? Apparently so.

When people go to a sports event, or go to hear a famous person speak, which seats do they pick? If people go to a concert or to a live theater, which seats do they want? Nothing but the best, up front, if they can afford it. Let the poor folk sit far back in the gallery! For such occasions, people want to be close to the action so they won't miss anything. But which seats do people favor when they attend a church worship service? Usually, first pick is not up front. Why is that? Why do people avoid the front rows in church? Is it any less important?

Jesus rewarded the faith of the four men who brought their friend to Him with the miraculous healing of his paralysis. It took four men in a team ministry to get their friend to the front row before Jesus. Indeed, one Good Samaritan couldn't have done what those four men did—no matter how much he cared. For this miracle, agreement and a mutual faith effort was required.

Years ago, even church people weren't thinking of the handicapped when they built church sanctuaries on the second floor. I remember attending a family reunion some time ago. There wasn't enough room for everyone to stay at the local relatives' homes, so our family checked into a bed-and-breakfast locally. On Saturday night of that weekend, I felt like taking a walk in the surrounding farmland countryside. My son, Mark, was the only family member who felt like coming along.

As we walked down a country road through a tiny village, we walked by an older, established church building there in the town. I remarked to my son, "Look at that church. Look at those steps." There must have been fifty steps ascending from the road up to the church building. I said, "How do they ever expect an older person or a handicapped person to get up that?"

The steps shot up and up, like Jacob's ladder. Finally, you reached the front door. It would take a four-man team ministry to get a person past that obstacle! The alternative to the steps would have been to climb the steep hill alongside the church and then come through the parking lot to the back door. As a result of church designs like this many people years ago just couldn't go to church and had to stay home as shut-ins.

Today many churches modernize old buildings by constructing handicap ramps so that even wheel chair people and the elderly, as well as people with heart problems, can conveniently come to worship. Some old churches with sanctuaries on the second floor have either added chair lifts or elevators. There is more thought now to making worship accessible to all. Even sound systems are installed that assist people with hearing impairments to hear all that is being said and sung. Restrooms are now designed to accommodate wheelchairs.

Team ministry faith thinks of people who can't get around well. Team ministry must also think of people who may look all right, but who are spiritually handicapped people. It must take into consideration the unseen suffering of those in great emotional pain or guilt, designing means for them to enter into worship comfortably as well.

The miracle of the forgiven and restored paralytic man is not only a celebration of awesome power and healing, but also a celebration of the faith of four men who had the daring to bypass any obstacle for the sake of a friend. Why? Because they had the team ministry faith to believe that Jesus could do anything.

Chapter Four

"Do What He Says."

The man called Jesus made clay and anointed my eyes and said to me, "Go to Siloam and wash;" so I went and washed and received my sight.

—John 9:11
Testimony of a healed blind man

The Gospel of John tells a story of light conquering darkness. One day, in the course of His active ministry, Jesus saw a man who had been born blind, who had lived his whole life in perpetual darkness. Day and night were the same to this man. He had never seen a human face, a beautiful sunset, or the street where his home was located. The beauty of flowers, birds, clouds in the day sky, and stars in the night were all veiled by a curtain of foggy darkness. Furthermore, this man's world of darkness kept him from reading, from the ability to work, from a life of independence.

In contrast to the man's darkness, Jesus described Himself to the blind man in the following way, just before He restored his sight: "As long as I am in the world, I am the light of the world" (John 9:5). And darkness met light on that momentous day! It was a darkness that had never before seen light. Can you imagine its beauty to this man?

Vision is such an important part of our lives that most people take it for granted. When vision becomes even slightly impaired, help is quickly sought from new eyeglasses or corrective surgery. What a joy to regain lost eyesight! But here was a man who had never seen *anything* before. For him to gain eyesight now, as a full-grown adult, would mean being introduced into a new world of vision. He would be able to see the children playing in the streets where he had only heard their voices and laughter previously. He would be able to see the food he had only smelled before and see *for the first time* the faces of his family and friends.

Just for a moment, think what it would be like not to be able to see. Close your eyes for a minute. If you drive a car, you can do it no longer. How will you be able to watch TV or read a newspaper? Will you be able to go shopping? Can you manage to give yourself personal care? What will you do without the help of someone else? A world of darkness can make one feel terribly alone. A blind person becomes a dependent person. Yet this is the daily life experience for many people.

When light comes to shatter the darkness, it is like liberation! And now the Light had come. Silently, Jesus spit on the ground and made clay. He then anointed the man's eyes with the clay and told the blind man the next thing he must do. Jesus made the first move, then gave directions to the man for the next.

Certainly, Jesus could have healed the man's eyesight instantly, but He didn't. Instead, He gave him a task to do that involved following specific directions. The instructions were to get himself to the Pool of Siloam and wash. We might say to him, if we could, "Do what he says." The blind man gave no argument. The Scriptures say, "So he went and washed and came back seeing" (John 9:7). He did exactly what Jesus told him.

If Jesus had the power to heal blindness, why did He then give a blind man responsibility to do something like washing clay from his eyes? For a very good reason: Following the directions of Jesus would be faith and obedience combined. When the blind man could see again, his testimony would now include his own cooperation with the Great Physician in following directives, forming an important model for others. When people asked the man how his eyesight was restored, he could honestly testify, "The man called Jesus made clay and anointed my eyes and said to me, 'Go to Siloam and wash;' so I went and washed and received my sight" (John 9:11). Can there be a lesson here about power and humility for us as well?

Faith *and* Obedience Are Sometimes Required

The Old Testament prophet Elisha gave similar instructions to a leper by the name of Naaman, an army commander. Elisha gave directions to Naaman to go and wash seven times in the Jordan River, which he reluctantly did, and was healed of his leprous disease. Naaman had protested that Elisha should just have waved his hand and cured the leprosy instantly without all the extra effort (II Kings 5:1–14). Yet he obeyed, and was made whole by God's power.

The blind man had been given a challenging task as well. Jerusalem's water supply was always a crucial concern. The Gihon Spring on the east side of Jerusalem

41

overlooking the Garden of Olives was essential. This water supply had to be secured from enemy forces if they ever came to attack the city of Jerusalem. In the Old Testament times a king by the name of King Hezekiah came up with the idea of digging a tunnel through rock to a lower level of the city, to the Pool of Siloam. The pools were like little reservoirs. The Gihon Spring was then sealed off so that it was hidden and the city's main water supply was secured.

Now Jesus is telling a blind man to go and wash in that specific pool, the Pool of Siloam. The blind man would somehow have had to find a way to get to that pool. He got there and washed, just as Jesus had told him to do, and he was no longer blind! For the first time in his life, he could see.

Normally, people think of spit as something to cough up and get rid of, as waste. It's not considered polite to spit, either. An historic church that I once served as pastor had a sign that used to hang in the church back in the 1800s. This vintage poster listed rules for the sanctuary, and one of them was: "No spitting of tobacco on the floor."

Here, Jesus spits in the dirt and then picks up the mixture of spit and dirt, anointing the blind eyes of the seeker with it. Now what could have been in that spit that would have the power to heal blindness? Was the power in the spit and dirt or in the man's faith? Or was the power in Jesus' touch? Did the blind man even know that Jesus had used His own spit to form an ointment for his eyes? Probably not. He couldn't see!

Once the blind man could see, there should have been only rejoicing and celebration by all. But then, as always, there were skeptics who questioned whether anything had really happened. Some regarded it all as a hoax. Even if the healing was authentic, grim religious critics questioned the timing of the restoration. They said it was the Sabbath and that was not the proper time to do the work of a physician, for to do so would be a sin. "Some of the Pharisees said, 'This man is not from God, for He does not keep the Sabbath.'" (John 9:16)

The religious critics, doubting that the man was born blind, checked with his parents to find out for themselves if he really had been. They immediately verified their son's lifelong blindness. But, not wanting to offend religious leaders, they referred them to their son for any more information on how the miracle had happened and who had done it.

The critics told the man that the person he said had healed him was not a good man, but was a sinner. Back and forth it went, the man's testimony and the skeptics' taunts. After all, displaying the power to heal a blind man presented a serious threat to religious leaders. Since many might follow such a miracle worker, this power might ultimately threaten their authority.

But the now-famous words of the healed blind man were hard to refute: "Whether He is a sinner, I do not know; one thing I know, that though I was blind, now I see" (John 9:25). The blind man felt that Jesus was a prophet. The religious authorities did not share that view. They were convinced that God had spoken to Moses, but not that He'd spoken to this Jesus.

What would it take to convince such hardened skeptics? The man who had just received his eyesight didn't need all the negative reactions to the miracle by religious leaders. He was just seeing the world for the first time! He could see the Pool of Siloam now for himself. He could see his parents, as well as the religious authorities who were questioning everything.

It is interesting to note that, in the Gospels, each time Jesus restored eyesight to some blind person He did it in a different way. Down in Jericho, where Jesus had given eyesight to Bartimaeus, it was Bartimaeus who'd cried out to Jesus for mercy. And Jesus hadn't given Bartimaeus any specific task to do for his healing. In his blindness, he had begged for mercy, and been healed.

Jesus attributed the response of healing to his faith. Jesus told the man, "Go your way. Your *faith* has made you whole" (Mark 10:52). Bartimaeus had requested that his eyesight be restored, and Jesus had directly responded to his plea. Jesus didn't put dirty spit on *his* eyes. Bartimaeus wasn't told to go to any pool to wash his eyes. It was an instantaneous miracle . . . right on the spot.

At Bethsaida, people brought a nameless blind man to Jesus, asking Him to touch him. This time Jesus took the man by the hand and led him out of the village. He spit directly on this man's eyes and laid His hands on him. The man could see better, but not perfectly. People "looked like trees," he said. Jesus touched his eyes again. Now the blind man could see clearly. In this case, it took a second touch. Why? Did Jesus have a reason for restraining His power so that the man would regain his eyesight gradually rather than instantly? Perhaps.

Jesus seemed to treat each person on an individual basis. Many Christians think God has to work the same way with every person. Some people think if you can't tell the very time and place you were saved, you haven't been born again. That's disturbing to authentic Christians who know the Lord but can't tell *exactly* when they were converted. Yet precisely because He *is* a personal Savior, God often works differently with different people.

My mother was a very committed, devout Christian who loved the Lord until the day she died. She told me that she couldn't point to a particular time when she became a Christian, because getting to know Him was so gradual and continuous a process. My dad, on the other hand, had a life-changing conversion experience at a Methodist men's meeting at Pen Argyl, Pennsylvania. My dad knew the time, the place, the moment of his salvation in Christ. Does it mean that my father's salvation was more real than my mother's? No. It was just *different*. Clearly, God works in different ways with individual personalities and particular life situations.

Getting back to the blind man who had his eyes rubbed with spit and clay by Jesus and was told to go wash in the Pool of Siloam; his situation was different. He was born blind. That's different than being born with vision and then losing it later. He had never seen the Pool of Siloam. Before this, the blind man was unable to have flashbacks of how things looked. If you or I close our eyes and are asked to describe how certain things look, we can do that easily. We can still visualize a living room, a kitchen, a house, a church, a car, faces, a cow, clouds, or stars in the sky.

Jesus would treat the man born blind in a special way. Jesus would do more than restore a physical function. Jesus would also restore the man spiritually. Did Jesus need the Pool of Siloam? Would the water eliminate blindness? Sometimes people think the water of baptism brings salvation. It's not the water that saves the person. It is obediently submitting to water baptism, submitting to what Christ said we must do if we are to be His disciples.

Obeying Christ's directives is what is important. If Christ says we should do something, we should do what He says, just as the blind man did. This means that Christ is not only seeking passive faith, but active, obedient faith as well. In this particular man's situation (of being born blind), Jesus was putting Him to the test. If he were to receive sight, He must first wash in the Pool of Siloam. Why?

Jesus restrained His power to heal instantly, which He had invoked on other occasions, for a worthy spiritual reason. The blind man would reinforce his own faith by doing what he was told to do. If you want to go to a physician, you should then listen to what the physician tells you to do, whether it is to change lifestyle, to take medication, to have tests, or to have surgery.

The blind man could not see Jesus before he was healed anymore than you or I can *see* Jesus today. But we can still hear or read Jesus' words and can sense Jesus' Presence— the same as the blind man did. Many people today who have good eyesight may still be spiritually blind. There is physical blindness and there is spiritual blindness. We all have blind spots. Some are in partial blindness spiritually; others are in total blindness spiritually. Yet both stand in need of Jesus' healing touch.

The world today seems to operate largely in spiritual darkness. As evidenced by the daily news reports, there is no shortage of hate and killing in our land. A New Testament writer described hateful people as those living in darkness, whether they are religious or not:

> But he who hates his brother is in the darkness and walks in the darkness, and does not know where he is going, because the darkness has blinded his eyes.
> —1 John 2:11

Even though the blind man's eyes were darkened, his sighted inner eyes of faith dared to follow Jesus' directive to go and wash in the Pool of Siloam. That act of obedience was the beginning of the way out of his darkness into the light. Notably, *spiritual* light preceded physical light.

Reputedly, Martin Luther wanted to take the letter of James out of the New Testament because of James' emphasis on works, as opposed to Paul's letters emphasizing faith. Yet in actuality, the two need to go together. James made that clear when he wrote: "So faith by itself, if it has no works, is dead" (James 2:17).

Notice that the blind man did *not* try to tell Jesus what to do. It was Jesus who instructed him. Nor did Jesus use power to force the blind man to go and wash in the Pool of Siloam. Jesus withheld His power until the blind man followed His directions. As a true leader, Jesus expected people to do what He said. He never forced His way on people. He expected His directions to be followed as a personal choice and decision by them.

Blessings of light and sight have always come from taking Jesus seriously and from doing what He says. Today, the world still sits in darkness. Yet things could be better if Jesus' instructions were taken more seriously and if the world's people would do what He tells us to do. Some do take Jesus seriously and do what He says, and *these* are the people who see the light. We read, for example, that:

> The people who walked in darkness have seen a great light; those who dwelt in a land of deep darkness, on them has light shined.
> —Isaiah 9:2

Likewise, those who refuse to obey God's directions for life continue to dwell in ignorance and darkness. Jesus *wept* over the city of Jerusalem because of its blind ignorance to the way to peace. Speaking to the city that God loved, He said:

> Would that even today you knew the things that make for peace! But now they are hid from your eyes.
> —Luke 19:42

Chapter Five

AN AMPUTATED EAR RESTORED

And one of them struck the slave of the high priest and cut off his right ear. But Jesus said, "No more of this!" And He touched his ear and healed him.

—Luke 22:50–51

Even the very disciples who walked with Christ on earth were often very ignorant of His ways and purposes. How it must have grieved Him to be so completely misunderstood by the men closest to Him. The Scripture illustrates this when, in Jesus' last miracle done on earth, He restores a victim of the violence done by one of His closest disciples.

This last miracle before Jesus' Crucifixion happened in the beautiful Garden of Gethsemane, which was located on the hill known as the Mount of Olives, overlooking the eastern wall of Jerusalem. Jesus and His disciples went there often. Following the Passover meal in the Upper Room, Jesus and His disciples went once again to that much-loved place. Here Jesus, knowing the ordeal that loomed before Him, could pray to His Father.

It was in this garden that Jesus was arrested by Roman soldiers, who had been led to the location by one of Jesus' own disciples, Judas Iscariot. Judas well knew where to look for the Master. When Jesus' disciples saw that they were surrounded by soldiers with swords and clubs—as well as hostile religious authorities determined to take Jesus away—they felt compelled to defend the Messiah with force. They asked Jesus if they could use swords. Luke's gospel records that one of the disciples cut off the ear of a man, a slave of the high priest. Jesus was horrified at such violence being perpetrated by one of His followers. *(John's gospel identifies Peter as the one who did the bloody act of violence in John 18:10.)*

Imagine the horrified victim holding the hurting and bleeding area where his ear had once been located! Jesus at once told Peter to put the sword away. Jesus wanted no violent force used to protect Him from harm. John's gospel missed an important part of the story, which is recorded more fully in Luke's gospel. John tells nothing about the restoration of the amputated ear. But Luke, "the physician," records a healing. One simple sentence says so much: "And He touched his ear and healed him" (Luke 22:51).

Modern surgery has done such wonders as reattaching a hand or an arm or a nose that has been somehow amputated. But this miracle was done before modern surgery and technology were known. Jesus just touched the ear and restored it on the man. It was Jesus' one last act of compassion before His trial and Crucifixion, one last reminder to his followers that they were *not* to use the sword. Conversely, amputation of a hand is common in the world of Islam where this is an accepted punishment for a person convicted of theft.

The slave of the high priest could now feel his ear again, in the place where it belonged. How did that happen? He must have wondered why Jesus would have done such a thing for him! What kind of man would do something like that at a time when He was being led away to judgment? The sudden pain and fright of losing an ear were gone.

This is the only *recorded* miracle of Jesus healing a victim of violence. But the likelihood of Jesus healing other such victims would come from this Biblical comment:

> But there are also many other things which Jesus did; were every one of them to be written, I suppose that the world itself could not contain the books that would be written.
> —John 21:25

Jesus' earlier parable of the Good Samaritan had taught people their responsibility to help victims of violence. So, Jesus was doing what He had taught. Even when His own life was at stake, He cared about someone else's ear. Even as He faced His own greatest challenge of obedience to God, Jesus had to undo what a misguided disciple had done. Isn't it interesting to note that only Luke, a physician, mentions Jesus' unique miracle of restoration? That day, the Garden of Gethsemane became a field hospital.

Today modern medicine seeks not only how to reattach body parts and to transplant body organs but also seeks ways to restore function to paralyzed people with spinal cord injuries. It has been inspiring to see people, such as the actor Christopher Reeve, injured in a horseback-riding incident, live positively, with the hope that someday they will be able to walk again.

An ear is such an important part of the body, not only for hearing, but also for cosmetic reasons. Newspapers covered a story in 1999 about a plastic surgeon from a Philadelphia hospital who went to the scene of an incident where an off-duty police officer had been assaulted, losing a piece of his nose. Frantically, friends searched for the missing piece that no one had been able to find. Turning over a crumpled newspaper and broken glass, he located the piece of the man's nose, rushed it to the hospital, then successfully reattached it to the officer's face! The surgeon remarked that it was easier to attach the missing piece than to reconstruct a new nose. Heroic acts such as this remind us of Jesus' caring example to us so long ago.

When I was a young pastor, I was walking to a parishioner's house during a blizzard. As I walked along the road, my ears became frostbitten, something I had never before experienced. It was scary. I thought I might lose an ear. At the same parish, I frequently visited an older couple in their home. The elderly husband was almost totally deaf. He had a large horn, which he would hold up to his ear. When I had something important to say, I had to get out of my chair, go over to him, yell down the horn, and ask, "Bill, can you hear me today?" And he would say, "Sure." Today people who are hearing impaired have wonderful, small hearing aids. Even churches have sophisticated sound systems that allow people with hearing difficulties to hear plainly wherever they choose to sit.

Much of Jesus' ministry was comprised of using His power to bring healing. Jesus made it very clear to His followers that He did not come to destroy, but to *save* and to restore life:

> The thief comes only to steal and kill and destroy; I came that they may have life, and have it abundantly.
> —John 10:10

Where did religious people ever get the idea that they should try to advance the Christian faith with violence and force?

Church history records countless tortures and deaths that were allegedly perpetrated to "defend" the true faith against heresy and to force religion on people by the sword through the union of church and state. Apparently, when Jesus told Peter to put the sword away, many of Christ's followers over the centuries didn't understand what He had said.

Peter was not the only disciple willing to use violence for the sake of the Christian cause. Earlier James and John wanted to bring down fire on a Samaritan village that did not want to welcome Jesus. They felt justified in seeking Jesus' blessing on violence, only to be turned down flat by Him. In fact, Jesus scolded them for entertaining such a thought:

> Lord, do you want us to bid fire come down from heaven and consume them? But He turned and rebuked them.
> —Luke 9:54–55

Oddly, religious people have for centuries been known to justify killing for the sake of their religion or to force particular beliefs on other people. Even in the modern world there are countless confrontations between Jews and Muslims, Muslims and Christians, Catholics and Protestants, Hindus and Muslims, Buddhists and Christians. Over the years, Christians have boldly persecuted other Christians— all in the name of Jesus, exercising power in all the wrong ways. Religious people have violently swung the sword, with its destructive power, all too often. Yet Jesus did not come to steal life away, but to bring life. He never advocated death for non-believers, but endeavored to change people and convert them by love rather than by the sword.

Jesus not only corrected Peter at Gethsemane; He also healed the wound Peter had inflicted. Refusing the protection of the sword, Jesus was then led away by His captors to a night of hearings and, finally, to His sacrificial death the next day. As Jesus had explained to His followers at an earlier time: "I am the Good Shepherd. The Good Shepherd lays down His life for the sheep" (John 10:11).

It seems that Christ does not bless *everything* His followers in churches do . . .

> For not with swords loud clashing, nor roll of stirring drums; with deeds of love and mercy the heavenly kingdom comes.
>
> —Ernest Shurtleff,
> hymn writer of *Lead On, O King Eternal,* 1887

How we defend our faith is all-important to our Lord. Not all methods will have His approval, as we have seen with Peter. Misguided zeal on behalf of strong religious beliefs and conviction can and *has* accomplished terrible things. Such zeal ordered the Crucifixion of the Savior and such zeal has carried out the death of many of His followers throughout history. Jesus predicted that this would happen when He said, ". . . indeed, the hour is coming when whoever kills you will think he is offering service to God. And they will do this because they have not known the Father, nor me" (John 16: 2, 3).

Some wonder why Jesus, if He had all power to heal, restore, and save men, did not save Himself from physical destruction. Was He powerless to do so? No. It wasn't that Jesus had no power to avoid the Cross. It wasn't because He was weak in power, or did not possess the power to save Himself. On that night when Jesus corrected Peter and undid his misguided deed, Jesus explained to Peter that He indeed had the authority and power to call for *legions* of angels to protect Him, should He choose to do so:

Do you think that I cannot appeal to my Father, and He will at once send me more than twelve legions of angels?

—Matthew 26:53

Jesus had all the power He would need, *if* He chose to use it. But He chose to submit to the Cross because it was His Heavenly Father's plan of salvation to overcome all the power of Satan.

People right up to the end mocked Jesus for what appeared to be powerlessness to come down from off the Cross. In His most agonizing moments, they mocked Jesus cruelly:

. . . save yourself! If you are the Son of God, come down from the cross . . . He saved others; He cannot save Himself. He is the King of Israel; let Him come down now from the cross, and we will believe in Him. He trusts in God; let God deliver Him now, if He desires Him; for He said, "I am the Son of God."

—Matthew 27:40–43

No, it wasn't that Jesus *couldn't* come down from the Cross; rather, it was that He chose not to. The doubters would have to go on doubting. No one, after all, was being forced to believe. Jesus absorbed the scorn of unbelievers, then died to save all who would choose to believe. Doubters will always ask, "Where is the power?" Believers will always see the power of Jesus' love in the healing touch of persons He has healed in body, mind, and soul. In the future, people would be won—not by the sword, but by an uplifted Christ:

". . . and I, when I am lifted up from the earth, will draw all men to myself." He said this to show by what death He was to die.

—John 12:32–33

See How Jesus Used Power!

Beyond human reason, this is the strange way God works His wonders of salvation through the power of the Cross. It is, truly, perfect in power:

> For the word of the cross is folly to those who are perishing, but to us who are being saved it is the power of God.
>
> —The Apostle Paul, 1 Corinthians 1:18

Chapter Six

The Faith Touch

Someone touched me; for I perceive that power has gone
forth from me.

—Luke 8:46

One day when people were crowding around Jesus, a
woman who had been plagued for years by an embar-
rassing ailment of continuous bleeding approached Jesus
from behind and just *touched* His garment. Immediately her
medical problem disappeared, and she was cured. For twelve
years doctors had been treating her without results. Now
healing came in an instant through merely her faith-filled
touch of Jesus' robe.

This woman didn't even have Christ's undivided attention. He had not said a word to her. His hands never touched
her body. He had not even yet seen her, yet a miracle happened. In the eyes of the religious institution, according to
Mosaic Law, she was considered "unclean" because of her
chronic bleeding. No, she could not help the fact of her

condition. It was not due to any sin or evil. Yet it was a "ritual uncleanness." The Law describes it as such:

> If a woman has a discharge of blood for many days, not at the time of her impurity, or if she has a discharge beyond the time of her impurity, all the days of the discharge she shall continue in uncleanness. . . .
> —Leviticus 15:25

No doubt it was difficult to get close to Jesus because of all the people crowded around Him. But this woman must have sensed the power Jesus had, and her faith compelled her to get just close enough to touch His garment. The combination of Jesus' reserve power and the woman's strong faith sparked healing for her. What doctors, for years, were unable to do, Jesus did without even trying.

Mark, in his gospel, adds some details about doctors that Luke's account doesn't mention. Possibly because Luke was a doctor, he didn't want to say negative things about physicians. But Mark's gospel tells how the woman got *worse* under her doctors' treatments, which also took away all her savings. The high cost of medical care without successful results!

> And there was a woman who had had a flow of blood for twelve years, and who had suffered much under many physicians, and had spent all that she had, and was no better, but rather grew worse.
> —Mark 5:25–26

Everyone knows that without adequate medical insurance the high cost of medical care today can drain resources dry. Modern technology has added to the cost, but also resulted in dramatic breakthroughs. For example, our son, Scott, has worked for years with ultrasound equipment. His company developed a new piece of modern technology that more accurately defined the different organs of the body. He invited my wife, Janet, and me to a demonstration of this instrument for the local medical community. As a lady lay on a table while the ultrasound equipment was defining the liver, the kidneys, and other organs, I asked the technician and sales person what this equipment would cost a hospital. The answer was $350,000. Yet physicians and patients alike felt that it was well worth it if people could be helped more effectively.

Yes, medical care costs a great deal, and it also saves lives. The woman who touched Jesus' garment bypassed technology and expensive medical care. Jesus never sent her a bill for what happened. She was well again, all because she had this belief that, "If I touch even His garments, I shall be made well" (Mark 5:28).

Jesus was the great physician that day. Ironically, He wasn't aware of the woman who came up behind Him. His presence was enough. He used no medicine, no surgery, no technology. Imagine power like that! Just to get near to Jesus must have been to feel His presence, His power, His all-encompassing love for people.

But Jesus did feel something when she touched His garment. He felt that someone was drawing power from Him. Isn't that remarkable? Instantly, Jesus stopped in full stride and asked the people, "Who touched my garments?" (Mark 5:3).

The crowd had no idea whom He was talking about. They said there was no way they could tell who had touched Him with such a large crowd of people all around. So Jesus looked around. Now the woman was nervous. She realized that Jesus was looking for her. She felt that surely she was in big trouble.

What would Jesus do to her if He found out she was the one who touched Him? She confessed she was the person. She fell down before Jesus and told Him the whole story, trembling with fear as she spoke. How would Jesus respond? What would He say, knowing that she had dared to touch His robe without His permission? Where had the woman found such nerve?

Astoundingly, Jesus praised her for her faith. She had done the right thing, he indicated. The faith touch of an ailing woman was rewarded with instant healing. Jesus' response was, "Daughter, your faith has made you well; go in peace, and be healed of your disease" (Mark 5:34). This woman might have been drained of financial resources, but she was not drained of faith resources, which she brought to Jesus and received of Him her healing. Jesus had so much power on reserve, ready to be tapped by the believing heart. The "woman with an issue of blood" had tapped into that power with her simple act of faith.

In other miracles of healing performed by Jesus, people came to him begging for help, or else He would notice people who needed help and minister to them. This story is different. Jesus never even *saw* the woman. She never asked Him for help. Hers was a silent cry for relief. Not a word was said and she was made well in an instant! The crowd never noticed what happened. But Jesus noticed something had happened. He quickly sensed that some of His reserve power had been drained off somehow by someone. How can we understand this?

People who live out in the country know what a water pump is. The new submersible pumps are so quiet you never know they are working. My first full-time pastoral appointment was to a small town that had wells and septic areas. Since I was raised in a city area, I didn't know anything about wells. In the parsonage basement there was a noisy water pump that you could hear whenever anyone was drawing water or flushing a toilet. That pump would start up with a boom: "Pah . . . boom-pah." Remember those old water pumps? The pump was always breaking down, and the plumber was always coming to fix it!

This story of the woman drawing power from Jesus is like the water pump. Jesus sensed someone was siphoning off power—just as someone would be drawing off water from a well. He immediately asked, "Who touched me?" He was asking this question, not because He was offended or angry. He wasn't being *touchy* because someone dared to touch His clothing without His permission. I think He wanted to know who it was that had touched Him so that He could recognize that person and his or her faith. He wanted to speak to that person, so He called out for someone to come forth. Frightened, the woman nonetheless obeyed. Now He could see the woman's face for Himself and speak words of assurance and peace to her and recognize her for her act of faith.

I'm sure you have famous heroes you would like to meet face to face sometime and shake their hands or get an autograph. It might be a famous athlete, a musician, a well-known political leader, or a Hollywood movie actor. It might be a famous religious leader, scientist, military leader, world-renowned leader, or author. Personally, I have always had the highest respect for Billy Graham. Years ago I attended a clergy luncheon in Philadelphia where hundreds of pastors had lunch with Billy Graham. I never expected to be able to speak with him. He surprised us by shaking hands with each pastor as we left. What a wonderful experience that was for me as he was giving us permission to shake his hand, have each of us look him in the eye, and speak to us.

Electricity is wonderful and necessary to our society. But you have to plug in to the power available. Out in Lancaster County, Pennsylvania, there are the Christian Amish people who choose not to use electric power. They live well without it, with lanterns and generators providing their minimal-use needs. They intentionally go *without* modern conveniences and TV. My wife and I were privileged to visit an Amish family when we lived in Lancaster County. We were on the family farm one day and went for a ride in one of their Amish buggies. I thought any minute a wheel would fall off or a car would run into us, but we got back safely.

Accessing electricity is not generally a problem in modern society. Still, even if one has electricity in their home, the circuit breaker has to be on and the appliances and lights plugged in for it all to work. Local churches are everywhere; Bibles are easy to obtain, and prayer is available to all. But believers have to plug into the power! Christ's power is great and is just waiting to be tapped. People have to get rid of negative thinking and choose to exercise faith. Do you need a miracle today? Catch up to Jesus and touch Him.

The "woman with an issue of blood" believed that Jesus was the answer. She wouldn't let any barrier or any crowd stand in her way. She believed that if she could but *touch* His clothing, she would be well again. Many people don't want to get fired up like that. She was going to be aggressive and work her way through the crowd to Jesus and touch Him without His permission. She never thought she would be noticed. She might have said to herself, "Who am I? *I'm a nobody.* What right do I have to go up to Jesus and ask Him for something?" Yet this story about an unassuming woman has been passed down through the centuries in the record of the Gospels. And we don't even know her name. Like the poor widow Jesus praised, the one who gave her small offering to the temple (Luke 21:1–4), she never thought she would be noticed.

If you want to get to Jesus badly enough, you'll work around all the obstacles or the crowds that get in the way and reach out to Him. Then, by your own act of faith, you'll be able to experience the power and healing this woman felt. The Holy Spirit will be released into your life. There is no telling what Jesus' power will do as it works in you or how your life will be joyously different when you reach out in faith to Him.

When a person comes to Christ at conversion time and becomes a born-again Christian, I think Christ notices that. That gets His attention. When a person says, "I'll follow you, Lord, wherever you want me to go; do whatever you want me to do," or, "I'm going to make a change in my life and follow you," I believe Christ notices that; you've got His attention. But if one just wants to play with religion and not get serious, I don't think He notices that at all. The Lord rejects as unacceptable any religion that is not authentic. The prophet Isaiah once wrote about God's displeasure with phony religion. He said:

> I cannot endure iniquity and solemn assembly . . . even
> though you make many prayers, I will not listen.
> —Isaiah 1:13, 15

Jesus didn't brag that He deserved all the credit for the woman's miraculous healing. Rather, He praised her for her remarkable faith, saying, "Daughter, your faith has made you well; go in peace, and be healed of your disease" (Mark 5:34). Her quiet faith had been the key. But of course, it was the Lord who rewarded her faith by exercising His great power.

Many who are sick or in pain or in some great, distressing trouble feel at times that the Lord doesn't know their plight, or that He doesn't care enough to change the circumstances. Rather than complaining, maybe people just need to become more daring and to reach out in faith, making active contact with Christ, touching Him in prayer, tapping into the healing power that He wants to share. Maybe the healing of the soul by His power will be even more valuable than the healing of the body, which is usually our first concern. God's response to our heart's cry is unpredictable, yet one thing is needful: to reach out and touch Jesus, and tap into His power. It is perfect, and He wants you to have it.

Chapter Seven

"IF YOU REALLY DON'T WANT TO KNOW, DON'T ASK."

"And I brought him to your disciples, and they could not heal him . . ." Then the disciples came to Jesus privately and said, "Why could we not cast it out?"
—Matthew 17:16, 19

Jesus had no sooner come down from the mountaintop experience of His glorious Transfiguration witnessed by Peter, James, and John—when the father of an epileptic boy knelt before him, begging for mercy for his son. Complaining about his frustration with Jesus' disciples, the distraught father stated that he was disappointed with them because they had failed to heal his son, who suffered terrible seizures that caused him to fall into the fire or into water. He must have heard how Jesus had given His disciples power to heal the sick and must have known that they did have many successes in healing the sick through their prayers, but not this time. He complained to Jesus, saying:

> And I brought him to your disciples, and they could not
> heal him.
>
> —Matthew 17:16

On this occasion, the disciples were ineffective. Here was a situation that they had no power to control. Here was a boy who didn't respond to their faith effort and prayers. What was wrong? Remember, Jesus was up on the mountain with three of the disciples when this request came. Did He have to be physically present for the prayer power to work? The disciples wanted to help the boy and respond to the father's request, but they found themselves unable to cure his epilepsy. Why?

Jesus had earlier given them authority to heal any disease. Matthew's gospel reminds us of their very important calling to aid the sick:

> And He called to Him His twelve disciples and gave them
> authority over unclean spirits, to cast them out, and to
> heal every disease and every infirmity.
>
> —Matthew 10:1

Now came the acid test, and the disciples felt helpless and embarrassed. Where was the power? What had gone wrong? Human need begged for help, and they couldn't do anything—not an unfamiliar situation for believers to be in, actually.

The famous sixteenth century Italian artist, Raphael, illustrated this pathetic scene of the defeated disciples, along with a portrayal of the Transfiguration of Christ, in the same painting. In this classic rendition of the event, the top of the picture shows Christ on the mountaintop in all His glory, conversing with Moses and the prophet Elijah, while Peter, James, and John have fallen to the ground in awed wonder at the sight of Christ's face shining like the sun and His clothing glowing white as light. The bottom of the picture is divided in half, one half depicting the epileptic boy and his family and community while the lower half shows nine helpless disciples.

For years, I have kept a small copy of this painting hanging on a wall in my study to remind me of this contrast of Christ's glory and the oft-frustrating weakness and ineffectiveness of the Christian church and its leaders. In all, twenty-seven persons can be counted in the painting. While three of the disciples remained up on the mountain as eyewitnesses of the wondrous, transfigured Christ and hearing, for themselves, God speak to His Son, the other nine disciples were not so privileged. They were down in the valley in big trouble. All nine had to admit defeat. It was doubtless a discouraging experience, a real *downer*, not to see victory and healing for the boy. They would be criticized for this, of course, by his father, who said, "And I brought him to your disciples, and they could not heal him" (Matthew 17:16).

At the same time, Peter would describe how he and James and John had just been eyewitnesses of the awesome Transfiguration of Christ on the mountaintop:

> . . . but we were eyewitnesses of His majesty. For when He received honor and glory from God the Father and the voice was borne to Him by the Majestic Glory, "This is my beloved Son, with whom I am well pleased," we heard this voice born from heaven, for we were with Him on the holy mountain.
>
> —2 Peter 1:16–18

Life is like that. While some Christians may be having mountaintop spiritual experiences at any given time, other Christians are down in the valley of life facing discouragement and defeat. Mountaintop experiences should inspire and encourage believers to maintain power in the valleys in order to effect change and to meet the needs of humanity, as well as to remain an over-comer in one's own personal life. Realistically, everyone has to come down off the mountaintop sometime, however, and face the challenges that lie in the valley.

Even Jesus and the three disciples who had been with Him on the mount had eventually had to return to the valley. And as soon as they came down off the mountain, there was the father of the boy, begging Jesus for help and complaining about the disciples' apparent "power failure." Matthew's account of what happened next is not as complete as Mark's gospel. While both accounts show Jesus' disapproving appraisal of the lack of faith in the disciples, Mark gives more details. He gives us Jesus' response to the father's report, which was to exclaim, "O faithless generation, how long am I to be with you?" (Mark 9:19). Matthew records that Jesus instantly healed the boy, providing no details how. But Mark's account shows how Jesus wanted to involve the father more.

Since the boy's father had been complaining about weakness of faith in others, now he would be put to the test as well. Jesus expected the father to show faith, whereas the father wanted to put the entire responsibility on Jesus alone. Notice that the boy's father said, ". . . but if you can do anything, have pity on us and help us" (Mark 9:22). Whereas the father had told Jesus, "if *you* can do anything;" now Jesus shifts the faith potential to the father by returning, "If *you* can!" Here is the exact quote:

> And Jesus said to him, "If you can! All things are possible to him who believes."
>
> —Mark 9:23

Wasn't this just like Jesus to give a person a partnership role in miracle working? By now the boy's loving father was ready to do anything to see his son healed. The words poured out of his mouth instantly, and almost without thought he said, "I believe; help my unbelief!" (Mark 9:24). If he could not exercise pure faith, without some doubt, then, with help from Jesus, this man believed that his weak faith could be reinforced. The father would believe as much as he could, but knew he needed help for the rest. Apparently his statement pleased the Lord.

Jesus commanded the unclean spirit of epilepsy to leave the boy. The evil spirit threw the boy into convulsions and then left. The boy looked dead, but Jesus took him by the hand and lifted him to his feet. The epilepsy was gone. The boy was well. His father had become part of the healing process. The power of faith was now a true reality to him. How could he ever forget this moment? His son, now well, would always be a reminder of this *hour of power*. The father had exercised all the faith he could muster, knowing that it might not be enough. But whatever he lacked in faith, he asked the Lord to supply. And look at the results!

All this upset the disciples, causing them to ask questions. They wanted to know why they had failed. What went wrong? Why is it that this father's faith went further than the faith of nine disciples of Jesus, who had been commissioned and empowered by Him to heal people? They came to Jesus later, when no one was around, asking why they had not been able to help the boy. Says Matthew, "Then the disciples came to Jesus privately and said, 'Why could we not cast it out?'" (Matthew 17:19).

Now if you don't really want to get an honest answer to a question, maybe you shouldn't ask it. In other words, *if you really don't want to know, don't ask.* In answer to their question, Jesus told them that they had failed because their faith was too small. Although they were Jesus' followers, they still lacked faith. How many churches would Jesus say this to today? How many Christian believers could stand up to Jesus' scrutiny of their faith?

How could the father of the boy demonstrate more faith than the apostles? What the father lacked, he asked to be supplied. Maybe it is a common thing for believers to need faith to be supplied where there are still doubts within themselves. Jesus told the apostles why they were unable to cast out the evil spirit, saying simply, "Because of your little faith" (Matthew 17:20).

The disciples didn't want to hear that they, of all people, lacked faith. Who wants to really know their own faults? Who wants to be told the reasons for their failings? Who wants to be made to feel uncomfortable in their religious standing? The disciples could have just gone safely on without asking what could be wrong with them. *If you really don't want to know, don't ask!*

Yes, the disciples had asked for it. And Jesus had given them an instant answer. He chided them for their lack of faith. If they had too little faith, how much faith would it then require? More than they had, obviously!

Jesus did not say a lot of faith was necessary. His answer was surprising. He said that faith "the size of a mustard seed" would do it. That's a very little amount! If little faith can move mountains, their faith must have been next to nothing on this occasion when they couldn't help the epileptic boy. Maybe our faith is next to nothing on too many occasions. Our little faith must be moved up a size . . . to what Jesus would have considered mustard seed size.

It is interesting to note that Mark's gospel account of Jesus' answer is different than Matthew's account. Mark makes no mention of little faith or to faith the size of a mustard seed being able to move mountains. Mark says Jesus answered the disciples' question by saying, "This kind cannot be driven out by anything but prayer" (Mark 9:29).

Intriguingly, Mark's emphasis was on prayer rather than faith. Actually, both emphases sound like Jesus. Maybe He said both. Faith and prayer certainly go together inseparably. The father's faith was a prayer asking for help. He said, "I believe; help my unbelief" (Mark 9:24).

In actuality, Jesus' reminder to His disciples of their lack of faith was like a call to arms. Jesus was not an information center, dispensing religious information. He was a *command center*. He gave directives, not advice. He gave commandments and mandates, not suggestions. The church must never settle for doling out religious information. The Church exists to put people in touch with Jesus Christ, God's powerful Son and to prepare people to hear Jesus' directives and to experience His power.

This brief account reminds us that we do well to ask, "Do people come to church as spectators or critics or to hear and obey the Word of God?" Each person must answer that question for himself. How much do we honestly invest of ourselves in worship and prayer? Do we really want to know what God expects of us today . . . what the will of God is for our lives? *If you really don't want to know, don't ask.*

A few may go up on some mountaintop and experience a Transfiguration of Christ. The rest of us will likely be surrounded with human need crying out for help in the valley. What can we do to help? Do we even want to know the needs of the hurting, let alone what God is expecting us to do to help them? To many, the problems of today's world seem so overwhelming and out of control. Frustrated believers still walk the earth, complaining about insurmountable mountains and inadequate resources to meet all the needs about us.

Maybe that is why Jesus referred to moving mountains by the exercise of *faith*. Can faith move the mountains of our time? Jesus called His disciples to be in the mountain-moving business. He promised that, with faith only as large as a tiny grain of mustard seed, believers would be able to say to any mountain, "Move from here to there," and it would move; and nothing would be impossible to them (Matthew 17:21).

But the mountains of life seem to stop most. Little goals seem more easily attainable. People settle for less than the highest. Great things don't get accomplished by setting safe, small goals. Faith dares to attempt to move mountains because God is being called upon to help. Faith and prayer go beyond human limitations! Faith knows that, as the angel Gabriel once said to Mary, who asked how she could bring forth a child though she had not known a man, ". . . with God nothing is impossible" (Luke 1:37).

Great things have often been accomplished in life because someone dared to believe that something could be done. The famous English Baptist missionary to India, William Carey (1761–1834), frequently encouraged Christians to go after greater goals and is quoted as having said, "Expect great things from God; attempt great things for God." As well, great insight and power has often come to those who have dared to ask God for an honest answer to why they were unable to move some mountain and attain their goals.

Faith is power! Jesus wanted to give power to His followers. Jesus was always tapping into power through His prayer life. His followers can—even today—tap into that same power through prayer and faith. Consider the limitlessness of this promise Jesus made:

> Truly, truly, I say to you, he who believes in me will also do the works that I do; and greater works than these will he do, because I go to the Father. Whatever you ask in my name, I will do it, that the Father may be glorified in the Son; if you ask anything in my name, I will do it.
> —John 14:12–14

Chapter Eight

CAN A DEAD MAN FOLLOW ORDERS?

And He said, "Young man, I say to you, arise." And the dead man sat up, and began to speak.

—Luke 7:14–15

What would it take to fill our churches with worshippers today? How can churches reach this challenging generation with the Gospel? And even if they could discover a way to do this, statistics show that it is increasingly more difficult to recruit enough pastors and priests for all the churches *presently* in need of leadership. Yet people's need of a place to worship and connect with God is today greater than ever. Clearly, it is time for a major revamping, not only of the local church, but also of theological education.

Specifically, how can the church of today reach a generation that appears indifferent to Sunday worship and Christian education? Many contemporary Americans, who can sit for hours watching television, reading novels and magazines, or checking the Internet until late hours of the night, cannot concentrate on a sermon for longer than ten minutes!

Some say that preaching is out of vogue and that Bible study is irrelevant to the modern world. A short, efficient service with little theology and *no* appeal for money or sacrifice is very popular in our time. Among church leadership, there is a temptation to make religion as easy as possible in order to attract more people. Yet what people really need may be something very different from what they want. The kind of costly discipleship Jesus talked about may not be popular in any age, yet following His way is always the greatest need of our souls.

In the Gospels, people were flocking to Jesus because something was happening! People were not just being talked to. People were not just singing choruses and listening to Jesus speak for ten minutes. What was happening was that sinners' lives were being changed and the sick and the lame were being healed and restored to health. Even the blind were made to see and the deaf could hear again. Lepers were cleansed; the crippled could walk again.

When Jesus walked the earth, there was joy and celebration in the air! His teachings were like treasures, making rich the spiritually hungry who surrounded Him. To add to all this, even the dead were being raised by this Jesus. Is that what it would take *now* to get people to take another look at the faith? Television cameras would certainly be focused on church activities if miracles were happening there and dead, empty churches were filling to capacity once again.

Miracles might help for a while, but even in gospel times people eventually strayed from Jesus—and some prominent religious leaders wanted Him dead. Even that generation long ago could not appreciate Christ. Would our generation, likewise, rise up to seek death for the Living Christ, who possessed such commanding power? Possibly. I'm sure many people would not appreciate His prophetic warnings, His exclusive claim to be God's Son, and His challenging invitation to costly Christian discipleship.

Still, miracles *are* happening today. People are being converted to new life in Christ by the hour worldwide. Quietly, yet wondrously, miracles of healing and deliverance are occurring every day. In God's natural order, every springtime represents a miracle of rebirth!

But it isn't often that the dead are raised. Death seems so final, and cemeteries are such quiet places. Can the dead rise? Can the dead ever hear again? Can a dead man follow orders? There is a beautiful story in Luke's gospel about a dead man who was ordered by Christ to rise from the dead. The young man in the story certainly followed the order to rise. This raises an interesting question: When a person is dead, can they hear anything? No, they are dead. They can't see, talk, or move in the grave. What can a dead person do? A dead person can't do anything in their old body. And yet the dead *were* raised by Christ's commanding power.

Resurrection Power

There are three stories in the Gospels where Jesus is found miraculously raising dead persons. He spoke to each of them and gave them orders to rise from the dead. One story is about Jairus' daughter, who had died of an apparent fever. Jesus went to her bedside and told her, "Child, arise," and she rose from her deathbed. Another story is about Jesus' good friend Lazarus, the brother of Mary and Martha. Jesus went to the tomb at Bethany and spoke these words loudly to the dead man, "Lazarus, come out." Lazarus came out of his tomb, still covered with all the grave clothes, which had to be removed from him by astonished friends and family.

The third story is about the young son of a widow whose body was being carried out of the town of Nain in a funeral procession. Jesus told the mother of the dead youth not to cry. As the pallbearers halted, Jesus gave orders to the dead man. He said, "Young man, I say to you, arise" (Luke 7:14).

In this case, we don't even know the young man's name. Jesus didn't call the stranger by name. He simply ordered him to rise. Then the Scripture says, ". . . the dead man sat up, and began to speak" (Luke 7:15). That would have been quite a shock to everyone there! The spoken word of Jesus was heard by the dead and life returned. Life and hearing must have been restored simultaneously. The man followed Jesus' orders, sat up—and even began to talk. How powerful the spoken word of Jesus was! The voice of the Master raised the dead. People of faith see this as a sampling of the future Resurrection, when God's people will all be raised from the dead:

> For the trumpet will sound, and the dead will be raised . . .
> —1 Corinthians 15:52

John the Baptist heard about this amazing event of the young man coming back to life at the command of Jesus. He immediately sent two persons to find out from Jesus if He really were the promised Messiah, for whom John was earnestly looking. Jesus gave them this message to carry to John:

> Go and tell John what you have seen and heard: the blind receive their sight, the lame walk, lepers are cleansed,

and the deaf hear, the dead are raised up, the poor have
good news preached to them.

—Luke 7:22

These deeds were the evidences of Jesus' power. All of
these things happened before modern medicine and technology. It could not be denied that Jesus had incredible
power and He was using it for good, to help people. He was
not using His power for His own gain or to destroy and
kill. He was not using power to force people to follow Him.
Jesus' powerful acts of mercy would be the proof that He
was the one who was to come and that there was no need
to look for any other. What more proof could anyone want?
Such power could only come from God.

The story of the resurrection of the young man is a very
short one, recorded with few details. In fact, the story is
told only by Luke. The other gospel writers missed this
miracle, apparently. In any case, there are more unknowns
in the story than knowns.

What don't we know? We don't *even* know the young
man's name. This is not so unusual for the New Testament
stories. Often names aren't given. We also don't know the
name of the youth's grieving mother, to whom Jesus spoke.
We do know she was a widow. We don't know the young
man's father's name. Where there are names given, they are
only first names, so even then it sometimes becomes difficult to tell one person from another if they both had the
same name. One way to tell more specifically who is being
referred to is to look for the mentioned that this person is
the son of a particular father.

But how would an obituary for this young man look?
Perhaps it would look something like this: "A young man
has died. His age is unknown. His parents' names are unknown. His father is dead. He and his family were from the

town of Nain. Occupation: unknown. Cause of death: unknown. It is also unknown whether or not he was married or had any children. He had no brothers or sisters. His religion is unknown. His moral character and reputation are unknown."

After the young man was raised from the dead, we still don't know much about what he did later. Did he go back to work? Did Jesus give him any directions? How was his life different after he came back to life? How could a dead man hear Jesus' command to rise from the dead, and what was that like? We don't know.

But we *do* know several important things from this brief story. We know the place where this all happened. Was the place more important than the man's name? What do we know about the place? Nain is in Galilee near Jesus' home, which was Nazareth.

Nain is also near another town called Shunam, in Galilee. Surprisingly, a similar resurrection miracle had taken place centuries earlier in that town. These are the circumstances: In the Old Testament, the prophet Elisha used to come to the town of Shunam to visit some friends, a rich lady and her elderly husband. They liked the prophet and offered him a room to stay in whenever he came to town. In return, the prophet asked the lady, "What can I do for you?" She told him that she wished she could have a baby.

Elisha gave the woman a prophecy. He told her she would have a baby boy. And miraculously, she did have a child some time thereafter. It was a boy, just as the prophet had said it would be. The son grew up, then suddenly died, causing his mother great anguish. How could this be? The miracle boy was dead. His distressed mother sought out the prophet again—this time barely shielding her anger and despair at her loss. Elisha prayed to God for the young man. Then he . . . *well*, the Old Testament says it best:

> Then he went up and lay upon the child, putting his mouth upon his mouth, his eyes upon his eyes, and his hands upon his hands; and as he stretched himself upon him, the flesh of the child became warm . . . the child sneezed seven times, and the child opened his eyes.
> —2 Kings 4:34, 35

This was more than mouth-to-mouth resuscitation. This was an incredible miracle. Elisha had *prayer power!*

Here at Nain, Jesus was using that same God-given power to raise a young man from the dead, just as Elisha had done centuries before in nearby Shunam. Is it merely a coincidence that in Galilee, quite near the same place the Old Testament prophet raised the youth from his death-bed, another young man is raised from the dead by Jesus?

We know other important things from the story of the miracle at Nain, things that tell us a lot about the Christ. Note that the young man's mother made no request to Jesus. She wasn't begging for Jesus to do something, to raise her son from the dead. Indeed, she had already accepted the fact of death. The funeral procession was her present reality.

It was a sad day and everyone was mourning. For a dead man to return to life was impossible. At the point of death, all knew, life was over. And the widow knew about death. She had already lost her husband. Now she had lost her only son, and she would be all alone. Was Jesus sad for the boy? No. He was sad for the grieving mother:

> And when the Lord saw her, He had compassion on her and said to her, "Do not weep."
> —Luke 7:13

The powerful Christ was also tender and compassionate. Without question, He loved people. Touched by her grief, Jesus would use His power to help her. Just so, power in good hands can often do immense good. Jesus stopped the procession. He touched the stretcher on which the dead man lay. He told the young man to rise, and instantly he sat up.

If you had been one of the pallbearers that day, how would you have reacted? The Gospel account says, "Fear seized them all; and they glorified God, saying, 'A great prophet has arisen among us,' and 'God has visited His people!'" (Luke 7:16). Would you not have been as afraid as they were? Power of this magnitude is indeed awesome.

Another known fact is this: After the dead man sat up, he started talking. Can a dead man talk? This one certainly could! Wouldn't you be interested to hear a speaker who once had been dead? Maybe churches would be full these days if we had people speaking who had come back to life from the dead. I wonder what the young man had to say. It's too bad Luke didn't choose to share that information with us. Luke himself wasn't an eyewitness to this event. He was not one of the apostles. He got his information from others who had been eyewitnesses, as he explained earlier in the introduction to his gospel.

This young man's resurrection was not permanent, as Jesus' resurrection was. This young man eventually died . . . *again*. After Jesus was resurrected from the dead, He ascended to His heavenly home. He was raised from death to life forevermore! And He is coming again. But the young man in this story will be raised for the second time, with all mankind, at the final Resurrection of the Dead, as is promised in the final book of the Bible, Revelation.

Isn't that exciting? Others who were raised from the dead also died again. That would also include all persons who were raised from their graves the day Jesus was crucified, when darkness came over the land and the curtain in the temple tore in two. Matthew's gospel account talked about an earthquake that occurred then, with rocks splitting and dead people coming up out of their graves:

> . . . the tombs also were opened, and many bodies of the saints who had fallen asleep were raised, and coming out of the tombs after His resurrection they went into the holy city and appeared to many.
>
> —Matthew 27:52, 53

Jesus is the only person whose Resurrection was permanent. The dead man followed Christ's order to rise. What does this mean? Jesus has the power to raise sinners from death of the soul for this life and for all eternity. That is *real* power. So, even death does not hold final power over His command. Jesus said:

> I am the resurrection and the life; he who believes in me, though he die, yet shall he live, and whoever lives and believes in me shall never die.
>
> —John 11:25

Chapter Nine

RELEASED FROM MADNESS

. . . and they came to Jesus, and found the man from
whom the demons had gone, sitting at the feet of Jesus,
clothed and in his right mind; and they were afraid.
—Luke 8:35

A homeless man had lost his sanity and was living in
the cemetery. If you'd lived in that time, you may have
found him wandering around naked among the gravestones.
He was strong and *could* be dangerous. Nor was he the type
of person grave visitors would want to meet on a dark night.
Chains could not hold him when he had demonic seizures.
He was a loner, living among the dead . . . someone you
would steer your child away from, and someone you would
not want for a neighbor.

The setting for this story would have been somewhere
along the eastern shores of the Sea of Galilee in the region
of the Gerasenes or Gadarenes; scholars aren't quite sure
exactly where.

Matthew's gospel insists that there were two madmen, while Luke and Mark say there was only one. Matthew says the two men were so dangerous that no one would dare get near them: According to the first account, ". . . two demoniacs met him, coming out of the tombs, so fierce that no one could pass that way" (Matthew 8:28). Whether it was one or two, you'll have to reconcile for yourself. Remember, Matthew would have been an eyewitness to these events since he was one of the twelve apostles, while Mark and Luke later recorded what they'd heard from eyewitnesses.

As earlier noted, Jesus and His disciples often crossed the Sea of Galilee by boat. This time they landed on the eastern shore, near where the madman was living. Luke's account says that the possessed man met Jesus as He stepped from the boat onto dry land. The man shouted at Jesus. He looked at Jesus as a tormenter. Although he was possessed, he recognized Jesus as God's Son right away. "What have you to do with me, Jesus, Son of the Most High God? I beseech you, do not torment me" (Luke 8:28).

When Jesus asked his name, the man told him it was *Legion,* because he was possessed by many demons. Straightway, the demons begged Jesus not to cast them out into space. Why the demons would beg to enter and possess a large herd of pigs is anyone's guess. Why Jesus granted them their request is also unknown. But Jesus did have the power to order the demons out of the man and somehow transfer them to the swine. This He did, releasing the man from his torment. Immediately, the pigs were infested with demon possession and they took off in a wild, crazed rampage. The demons caused the pigs to run madly down a steep bank into the water below it and they all quickly drowned. The whole story sounds so strange to modern ears!

As we can see, there was a lot of power being exerted here by Jesus in order to deal with a "legion" of devils and free the tortured man. Imagine how the pig herdsmen in the area reacted when they saw all the dead pigs floating on the water, their very livelihood now lost! Naturally, the local Jews wouldn't have minded because Mosaic Law pronounced swine as "unclean" animals, unfit to eat. No self-respecting Jew would be found raising such animals; that would be left for Gentiles to do.

The herdsmen ran to tell the rest of the community what they had seen. When the community came and saw for themselves the change in the man, who was now in his right mind, they were afraid. The man was wearing clothing and was acting and talking normally. The demons were gone from him; he was a new man . . . no longer a threat to the community. Whatever happened? How could Jesus have the power to do something like this? This was not the result of years of psychiatric therapy or of good institutional care. It all happened so suddenly. Jesus had simply commanded the unclean spirit to leave the possessed man. Jesus had exercised power over a legion of demonic spirits. His strong power forced the demons to leave. *That indeed is power:*

> . . . and they came to Jesus, and found the man from whom the demons had gone, sitting at the feet of Jesus, clothed and in his right mind; and they were afraid. . . .
> —Luke 8:35

To the astonishment of all present, Jesus even had a cure for mental illness! The man had identified himself as a man possessed by a battalion of demons controlled by inner voices. The spirits inside him had driven him out of control. Yet at the Lord's command, His oppressors had to leave, setting him free.

The Bible talks very frankly about demons and demon possession, presenting it as a very real occurrence in Jesus' time. Even today, how else can one explain so many crazed acts of violence in our society? How can people do some of the horrible things that they do to other people, those un-thinkable things that we hear of every day in the news broad-casts? In questioning, the perpetrators of these crimes often tell how they heard inner voices telling them to kill some-one, the irrepressible voices of unclean spirits from the in-visible spirit world.

So often great power rests in the hands of possessed people. Satan controls many wicked rulers. The name of Adolph Hitler sends chills through anyone who has seen what one dictator can do in the destruction of millions of lives. But that is only one name. History is full of powerful rulers who have been under satanic control!

When I was in Israel, I was amazed to hear several dif-ferent speakers talking about the demonic, about an evil spirit in the land. Frankly, I wasn't expecting to hear an emphasis on that subject in the Holy Land. But it's evident that an evil spirit certainly keeps peace at a distance in that part of the world, where many stir up hatred and division. Certainly, it is frightening to see a bomb or a gun in the hands of a person who has gone mad, who seems possessed.

Matthew and Luke don't tell us how many pigs received the evil spirits cast out of the man, then perished in the water. Mark states that it was two thousand (Mark 5:13). That's a lot of pigs! The spirits in one man sent two thou-sand pigs wildly out of control. Think what they were do-ing to that one tortured man! When the military resources of a nation or empire are in the hands of one madman controlled by demons, one of Satan's servants, untold desolation can definitely result.

Jesus had restored a possessed man. But the people feared Jesus so much they requested that He leave their community. They feared what they could not understand. There was power in the hands of Jesus and they sensed it. What might He do next? Whose animals would be lost next? What might He do to other people? Where did Jesus' power come from? There were too many unanswerable questions for the people to rest concerning Him. He had to leave. He was no longer welcome, even though a wonderful miracle of restoration had just happened.

When the restored man saw that Jesus was leaving, he asked to go with Him. But Jesus directed the man to return to his own community and tell his people what God had done for him.

> "Return to your home, and declare how much God has done for you." And he went away, proclaiming throughout the whole city how much Jesus had done for him.
> —Luke 8:39

The hope now for that community would be one restored man who could tell how Jesus had released him from his mental illness and demonic possession. This man would be an evangelist for Jesus, just like the other disciples. He just couldn't get into the boat and leave with Jesus and His followers. He would stay home and be a witness there of Christ's power to transform life. The former homeless man would no longer wander naked and aimless around the graves of the dead. He had found new life in Christ, and was a *walking miracle!* The chains of demonic possession were broken. He was living evidence of Christ's miraculous power.

Even as Jesus would no longer be welcome in that community in spite of the good He had done with His spiritual power, so He would not be welcomed today in every community, board room, or government gathering. He would not be welcomed into every synagogue, mosque, temple, or even into every church.

But Jesus had landed one convert in that town. Or, if Matthew's account was right that there were two madmen, then Jesus had doubtless converted two. But even just one or two witnesses for Jesus can change an entire community. It doesn't take a great number of Christians to make a convincing difference if those Christians are really dedicated to Christ and can demonstrate transformed lives as His followers.

Sometimes it seems that a whole society can get sick due to an unhealthy belief system. Today, madness is increasing in the land. More shocking horrors are added to the bad news each day—everywhere in the world. One asks how people can be so cruel and can do the terrible things they do . . . torturing, oppressing, bombing, shooting, slaughtering people as if they had no value. "Has the world gone mad?" is a common question after each shocking, unexplained incident which seems to "top" all previous ones.

Yet, if Jesus could bring healing and restoration to possessed individuals, can He not restore entire societies to sanity? When the Kingdom of God comes, the madness will end. Hatred will be a curse of the past. Jesus' way of love and healing will be the rule of the land. In His lifetime, Jesus wanted to show us the power love has to heal and transform. And when He comes again, sanity will be restored under the loving, orderly rule of God.

In the meantime, individuals who have been renewed and restored by Christ must shine as lights in a darkened world. Followers of Christ, filled with the Holy Spirit of God, are the designated agents of that power from on high through which God cleanses and saves others.

Now to Him who by the power at work within us is able to do far more abundantly than all we ask or think, to Him be glory in the church and in Christ Jesus to all generations, forever and ever.

—Ephesians 3:20, 21

Chapter Ten

"NOW THAT HE HAS TOUCHED A LEPER . . ."

"See that you say nothing to anyone; but go, show yourself to the priest, and offer for your cleansing what Moses commanded, for a proof to the people." But he went out and began to talk freely about it, and to spread the news, so that Jesus could no longer openly enter a town. . . .

—Mark 1:44, 45

J esus was always reaching out to the untouchables of His society. There were the tax collectors and the Samaritans. There were the sinners. Then there were the lepers. The lepers were viewed as contagious threats to the health of the community and were forced to live in isolation outside of the populous areas. No one was to get near them or to touch them. They were not welcome anywhere. They had to dress a certain way, with torn clothes, for identification. Further, they were to cover their upper lip and announce their presence with the words, "unclean, unclean."

Imagine how everyone would step back when such an announcement was made—to avoid the diseased person.

This was social ostracism in its most brutal form. Because of the incurable nature of this dread disease, lepers evoked fear everywhere they were seen. Such isolation could destroy self-esteem. I remember when I was a boy I got the usual childhood diseases like the measles, whooping cough, mumps, and chicken pox. At such times, there would be signs posted on the outside of our house showing that it was under "quarantine," and no one was to enter it.

When someone in an office or at a store has a bad virus and is coughing and sneezing, people tend to want to keep their distance to avoid getting the germs passed to them. Many times as a church pastor, I would be called upon to visit someone in a hospital who had an infection and would be told by hospital attendants to don a gown, put on a mask, and not to touch the person in bed. I couldn't shake their hands or give them a hug as physical contact would spread the infection to me and to everyone I would come into contact with thereafter.

Mark's gospel tells how a leper once came to Jesus on his knees, begging Him to make him clean. The leper believed Jesus had the power to heal his leprosy if He chose to do so. And Jesus did choose to remove the dreadful disease and make him whole. Mark's gospel adds that Jesus was "moved with pity" for the man. Matthew and Luke in their gospels missed that little comment. But that sounds like Jesus. As always, He had a real concern for suffering people, especially for the "rejects" of society.

Tax collectors were hated by the people, yet Jesus visited the home of Zaccheus, a rich tax collector, after He found him sitting up in a sycamore tree, trying to get a look at Him as He passed by. Samaritans were also on the untouchable list. Yet Jesus' most famous parable was about a

Good Samaritan. His later encounter with the Samaritan woman at the well is a familiar story to most as well.

Sinners themselves were shunned by the religious leaders of Jesus' day, who were always offended by the Master's habit of associating with sinners, even eating and drinking with them. Is that surprising? What would modern Americans think of Jesus if they would see Him associating with those people regarded as the untouchables of our generation? But Jesus *expected* His followers to visit people in prison, to visit the sick, to feed the hungry, to offer clothing to the needy, and to welcome the stranger. His parable of the Last Judgment tells about the separation of the sheep from the goats on the basis of whether or not people reached out to the needy, whomever they were (Matthew 25:31–46).

The leper was a reject of society, one of the untouchables, isolated from family and friends. Because Jesus was moved to pity the man, He did an unthinkable thing. Jesus reached out to the leper and touched him. He had no mask on, nor gown, no gloves to protect Himself. This alarmed those who saw it. After Jesus had touched the leper, would *you* want to have been the next person He would touch? Or would you have said to Jesus, "Would you mind washing your hands well before you touch me?"

Now that Jesus had touched the leper, He seems to have created a problem. It is true that the man's leprosy was healed. But who knew that for sure? That is why there was a requirement for a person cured of leprosy to go to a priest and be examined, then offer sacrifice, and go through a waiting period before he was finally pronounced clean. Mark's gospel says that the man's leprosy was cured "immediately." Jesus must have had a reason to touch the leper. Jesus told the restored man not to tell anyone how the miracle happened. That would create problems Jesus wasn't looking for.

Jesus told the man to go to the priest first and go through the cleansing ritual proscribed by the Law. Then he would have the necessary proof that indeed the man was well again. Then people could believe the miracle. But the man didn't listen. He was so excited he began to spread the news that he was cured and that Jesus had performed a miracle, when so far there was no proof of a miracle. Mark's gospel states that now Jesus could not show Himself freely in town. He couldn't go into town since He had touched a leper. He stayed out in the country, but people came to Him anyhow since He couldn't come to them. Jesus had touched an *untouchable*. The former leper could not contain his joy and gratitude. His low self-esteem had been lifted to the sky because of Jesus' touch.

Most Christians have been taught to share the Gospel, to tell others about Jesus and the salvation available through Him. Here, however, Jesus was instructing silence. It was all too hard to understand. Wouldn't the directive to be silent be a relief to many modern church people who don't like evangelism, who want to keep their religion to themselves and not feel pressure to share it with others? Many modern Christians find it hard or awkward to talk about Jesus Christ as Savior, or even to invite someone to attend church. Jesus' instruction to keep silent was just for this particular man. He was told *first* to do the ritual required by the community and the Jewish religion. There is always a proper time and place to witness to God's grace in Jesus Christ; likewise, zeal can do damage when it is misplaced.

Still, you have to understand how the healed leper must have felt. He was suddenly free of his miserable disease. He probably felt young again and ready to tackle the whole world! He would be able to go back into town, live his life, and go to work again. He would no longer be an outcast. Even if it had not yet been proven to the satisfaction of the community, he knew he was well! He wanted a *shortcut* to the Mosaic requirements.

The Law of Moses was a constant awareness in this man's society. He knew he was supposed to go to the priest; that he was to bring two live birds. He understood that one bird would be killed and its blood sprinkled on the live bird. That the blood from the live bird would be sprinkled on the leper seven times. Then, still, no person could enter his home or tent. He would have to wait outside the home for seven days. Then another sacrifice was to be brought in, and *then* the priest would declare a clean bill of health. Only then could the town accept the previous outcast into society and touch the one who had been untouchable.

If the leper were to go back into town without doing this, then go all over town saying, "Jesus healed me, I'm well," no one would believe all his talk about religion. He hadn't gone through the necessary process. And there was good reason for doing so. . . .

Premature religious talk can turn people away from the faith rather than convince them of God's reality. Many don't want to hear the testimony of some persons because their words are contradicted by their lives. A word for that is *hypocrisy.* Some people are all talk and no action, all fluff and no substance. Jesus was concerned about the healed leper giving testimony before it was time. Such a premature witness would only hinder His ministry to that area. He would no longer be able to enter into town freely.

In the eyes of the community, the former leper was still an untouchable. Jesus had touched him and exposed Himself to the dread disease, which He might pass on to others.

The testimony of the healed leper, without obedience to the Law and Jesus' own command to fulfill it, would be regarded as a false claim without proof. Fear ruled out any assurance that the claim was true. But the man's testimony must have convinced some, because Mark's gospel tells us that even though Jesus had to stay out of town, "people came to Him from every quarter" (Mark 1:45).

In the New Testament, there was the same hesitation to believe some testimonies of new converts. Take the convert, Paul, who before his conversion had hated Christians, and had brutally persecuted the Early Church. He gave his consent to the stoning of Stephen and even held the garments of those killing this church deacon. Later, Paul announced his conversion to Christianity, but the church was still afraid of him. To be believed, another man had to come to Paul's rescue. It was Barnabas who gave proofs of Paul's life-change to the community and showed that Paul could now be trusted in spite of his past persecution of believers. Because he had come to know Jesus, "all things were made new," even within this notorious persecutor of Christ's followers.

When Chuck Colson, imprisoned for his role in the Watergate scandal, "got religion," many did not believe it. But it was nonetheless real. His decades-long prison ministry is a modern day testimony to a very real conversion experience. The point is that people frequently doubt miraculous events of this kind, even today.

Sometimes it may appear, when reading about Jesus' healing miracles, that physical health and restoration was His main concern. Was His mission to be a physician of the human body, or was there more to it? Jesus must have spent the bulk of His time in ministry healing people brought to

Him in countless lines. Even in the gospels we read of His fame, gained from performing physical healings:

> So His fame spread throughout all Syria, and they brought Him all the sick, those afflicted with various diseases and pains, demoniacs, epileptics, and paralytics, and He healed them.
>
> —Matthew 4:24

Jesus wanted to assure John the Baptist that He was the promised Messiah by virtue of the evidence of such physical, medical restorations:

> Go and tell John what you have seen and heard: the blind receive their sight, the lame walk, lepers are cleansed, and the deaf hear, the dead are raised up, the poor have good news preached to them.
>
> —Luke 7:22

Small wonder that, wherever Christians have taken the church into the world, medical missions has usually been some part of the endeavor. Even local churches have a concern for the sick in the parish, and part of pastoral ministry is visiting the sick in homes and hospitals. Prayers for the sick remain an important part of the ministry of local congregations.

But Jesus also said to tell John that "the poor have good news preached to them," as a sign of His identity—along with medical miracles. Jesus came to do more than heal sick bodies. He came to restore the souls of people. He came to offer them salvation and eternal life. He came to preach good news to the poor:

99

> I must preach the good news of the kingdom of God to other cities also; for I was sent for this purpose.
>
> —Luke 4:43

The reason Jesus used His God-given power to heal people's bodies was because He cared about people. Because He loved people, He used his power to help them to regain their lives and to find joy again. Because He loved the total person, He would help them find salvation for their souls and minds as well as for their bodies. People needed God. They needed salvation, forgiveness, hope beyond the grave, comfort, direction out of their lostness, love, healing, and peace. They needed a Savior and a Lord.

Healing of the body, then, was not Jesus' total ministry; it was a vital part of His ministry, but not His entire ministry. If Jesus had never healed anyone, it would indicate that either He didn't really care about people and their hurts or else He lacked sufficient power to do anything about them. Jesus both cared for people and He also used His power for good. He saw people who were sick and hurting and He could do no less than reach out to them to perform the merciful wonders that He did. His medical miracles have been known worldwide since then and have inspired the creation of hospitals and medical facilities in countless places by caring people who have become part of the healing team, emulating their Master.

What is the real ministry of the local church? So often churches become successful in one phase of ministry and their church is identified with that phase only. But each church must be diligent not to let any peripheral ministry detract from the centrality of the ministry of that which the church has been called to do: to proclaim the Gospel of salvation through Christ and offer healing and evangelization of the world. Churches must be careful not be so distracted by *busyness* with peripheral ministries that their main mission is lost. Christians who rightfully pray for the healing of the sick must not forget to pray also for salvation and healing of the soul.

Conversely, Christians who pray for salvation must also pray for the healing of the sick. Jesus died on a cross to save sinners. The world is sick and needs the Great Physician for healing. Keeping these two priorities in dynamic balance is so important. When Jesus was criticized for dining with sinners and tax collectors, He gave this explanation for it:

Those who are well have no need of a physician, but those who are sick; I have not come to call the righteous, but sinners to repentance.

—Luke 5:31, 32

We all have sinned and have needed salvation. As sinners, we were the outcasts, the untouchables. In Christ, we have found forgiveness and wholeness. Christ has set the believer free. Liberation is a joyful experience, which makes one want to tell the whole world that Jesus made it all possible! You don't have to be silent. You can communicate your faith. In fact, you must, if you care about people as Jesus did. But the world *will* want proof that you have been cleansed of the disease of sin, that you have experienced forgiveness. A phony life with wordy testimonies won't do for this generation.

Only a life of integrity and love will be persuasive. Probably fewer people are persuaded by argument than by love. The world about us is full of rage, fear, and doubt. It will take a lot of love and caring to draw out responsive faith from the skeptics and hostile scorners of the Gospel message. It will take a lot of integrity and much less hypocrisy to convince a *doubting but questioning* age which fears genuine religious commitment.

The sacrament of Holy Communion reminds each believer that salvation has brought healing and joy to the soul. God loves and forgives us. Paul's letter to the church at Rome says it so well:

> But God shows His love for us in that while we were yet sinners Christ died for us.
>
> —Romans 5:8

Yes, while we were untouchables, Christ reached out, touched us, and made us whole.

Chapter Eleven

"POWER TO GOD'S PEOPLE!"

Now many signs and wonders were done among the people by the hands of the apostles . . . The people also gathered from the towns around Jerusalem, bringing the sick and those afflicted with unclean spirits, and they were all healed.

—Acts of the Apostles 5:12, 16

We normally think of Jesus doing all the healing miracles in the New Testament times. It is often forgotten that Jesus shared His power with His disciples. He authorized them to go out and heal the sick just as He was doing. The Gospel account of Luke reminds us that Jesus not only sent the twelve out to help Him and to preach, but that Jesus also sent them out to heal:

And He called the twelve together and gave them power and authority over all demons and to cure diseases, and He sent them out to preach the kingdom of God and to

> heal . . . And they departed and went through the villages, preaching the Gospel and healing everywhere.
>
> —Luke 9:1, 2, 6

When I was ordained into the ministry, as I put my hands on the Wesley Bible, the bishop's hands and hands of other pastors were laid on me with the words, "Take thou authority as an elder in the church to preach the Word. . . ." The "laying on of hands" at ordination has been a longstanding tradition of the Christian Church. As well, pastors in active service soon learn that a large part of their ministry is not just preaching but also visiting the sick and offering up prayers for their healing.

Preaching and healing have somehow always gone together. I once heard a Roman Catholic priest at a hospital clergy seminar remark that every Mass was a healing service. All Christians need to realize that there is healing in the act of worship itself.

If Jesus used His power to heal the sick, why shouldn't the followers of Jesus do the same, if they were given the power to do so? Followers of Christ who take Him seriously will see that Jesus wanted to pass on the spiritual power for healing to His followers. Jesus even prophesied that His followers would not only be able to duplicate what He was doing but could expect to see even greater things done by believers:

> Truly, truly, I say to you, he who believes in me will also do the works that I do; and greater works than these he will do, because I go to the Father. Whatever you ask in my name, I will do it, that the Father may be glorified in the Son; if you ask anything in my name I will do it.
>
> —John 14:12, 13

Naturally, when we exercise this power in Christ's name, it will still be the Lord Jesus doing the healing. But His followers who are genuine believers will be used by the Lord to do what Jesus did—and more. Jesus was giving power to God's people for the benefit of all humanity. Healing should not just be a fringe experience of tent crusades, but should be central to all churches. Prayer vigils, prayer chains, and prayers for the sick have to make a difference for others. If the apostles were not always successful in seeing their prayers bring healing, such as their failure with the epileptic boy, then modern Christians must not stop praying if they don't always see immediate success. It is so easy to get discouraged with prayer when results aren't seen. Christians often feel so powerless and conclude that their churches are ineffective, yet it is not so! People are being healed—physically and spiritually—through believing faith today.

I once had a man who said he was a Jehovah's Witness visit me. We got to talking about Jesus' healing miracles. He commented, "Well, this is not the time of healing miracles anymore. That only happened in Bible times." I said, "You're wrong. You need to go back and look at what the Gospels say." Jesus did not limit healing to the Apostolic age, to gospel times, not when He said, "Truly, truly, I say to you, he who believes in me will also do the works that I do . . ." (John 14:12).

That's about as plain as plain can be. In making this statement, Jesus implied that this was just the beginning of miracles. His followers would not only continue His healing ministry, but they would be able to accomplish even greater things than He had done. He said, literally, ". . . and greater works than these he will do . . ." (John 14:12).

When you stop and think about it, Billy Graham, Pope John Paul II, Dr. Robert H. Schuller, Mother Teresa, and

Dr. Martin Luther King, Jr., have preached to millions more people than Jesus ever did in His three-year ministry. With television and radio, the Internet, and other means of mass communication, the potential for reaching millions all around the world is limitless. Think of the healings made possible by modern medicine through healers who were inspired by the Great Physician!

Jesus' ministry of preaching, teaching, and healing took place within only a three-year period. Before He began His ministry at thirty years of age, He was a carpenter in the small town of Nazareth. Jesus had to do what many today are forced to do: change careers. He exchanged His career of carpentry for that of a teacher, preacher, and physician of the body, mind, and soul.

Jesus' disciples also underwent career changes in order to follow the Great Physician. Former fishermen exchanged their fishing nets for a new career in "catching people" for the Master. A former tax collector would now be taught how to offer salvation to people rather than collect money from them. The other disciples had to leave other careers to follow a new Master.

After Jesus' resurrection, He ascended to His home in heaven. Now what would the disciples do since Jesus was gone from them? Would the wonderful healing miracles end? No. The Acts of the Apostles in the New Testament says that the miracles continued being performed by Jesus' apostles after Pentecost.

> Now many signs and wonders were done among the people by the hands of the apostles . . . The people also gathered from the towns around Jerusalem, bringing the sick and those afflicted with unclean spirits, and they were all healed.
>
> —Acts of the Apostles 5:12, 16

Although Jesus' presence was no longer seen visibly, yet Jesus was working through His disciples—the same as He works through His Church today.

The fisherman apostle, Peter, performed the first specific healing miracle recorded in the Acts of the Apostles. A man crippled from birth begged for money as Peter and John were entering the temple in the afternoon for prayer time. The cripple really expected to get money from the two disciples when Peter told the man to look at them. Peter got his attention, then told the man he didn't have any money to give him. Instead, Peter offered the cripple something far better than money. The cripple didn't go home financially richer that day. But he *was* able to walk home instead of being carried by other people. Those famous words of Peter still resound throughout Christendom: "I have no silver and gold, but I give you what I have; in the name of Jesus Christ of Nazareth, walk" (Acts of the Apostles 3:6).

Next, Peter took the man's right hand and raised him up to his feet, and there was an immediate strengthening of his feet and ankles. Do you wonder why the man not only walked but leaped around and praised God? How could Peter have had such power? How did he do it? Wasn't this the disciple that people remember for denying that He even knew Jesus the night before the Crucifixion? This is a different Peter, a restored disciple, who was now helping to restore another man who was born crippled!

Peter acknowledged that he didn't have economic power. He had never been a rich man. The former fisherman, a "man's man", was also the Lord's man. Because he was the Lord's man, he had another kind of power, spiritual power, which had been given to him by God's Holy Spirit, the same kind of power that Jesus had.

As a result of this healing miracle by Peter, other people came, bringing the sick from towns all around Jerusalem.

And they were healed. Doesn't that sound exactly like the gospel stories of Jesus healing people and crowds bringing the sick to Him? What we have with Peter and the cripple is an example of "copycat" power, a believer copying what he had watched Jesus do so many times in restoring other cripples.

We hear so much in our society of "copycat crimes." These criminals are inspired to do an evil thing in real life that they copy from some film story . . . or reenact evil acts they see portrayed on the news. Why are people so prone to copy evil and so little inclined to copy good behavior? Thank God for the Apostles, who copied the good use of power by Jesus to care for people and to heal people's bodies. Jesus inspired His followers to continue what He'd started.

Road rage is a problem on our highways today. It wasn't always like that. But road rage is the result of copying bad, selfish behavior, reflecting the insensitive "me first" attitude of so many today. People with expensive, powerful autos sometimes want to show off their power under the hood by darting in and out of already fast-moving lines of traffic to get ahead of someone else, threatening everyone who is in the way.

People can choose to copycat good or evil. Here is a silly example from my experience as a pastor of a church in New Holland, Lancaster County, Pennsylvania. For some time while living there, I'd been having intermittent pain in the chest area. My doctor, who was a faithful member of the church and a good friend, advised me to buy a bicycle and to get more exercise to relieve stress. I bought a brand new red Schwinn bike, which I treasured. After meetings at night, I would race the bike up and down the roads through the farmland countryside. I had a generator on the bike for lighting. The faster I went, the brighter the light got! I would race by cows and horses, pigs and chickens, then return home feeling great. My chest pains went away, thank God.

I soon started to ride the bike when I went out to visit people. Then I used the bike to go to the Kiwanis Club meeting at the local diner. All the other men were coming to the luncheon with their nice, fancy cars while I would pull up to the diner on my bike, chain it there in front, and go in to lunch. A number of months went by and soon there were a whole lot of other bikes tied up in front of the diner—copycat riders, all of them. And I received no commission for any bikes sold. I think that was good copycatting. Exercise is good for you, after all.

The young and old among us copycat the fashions of the time. Even children have their fashion standards to copycat, whether it be the brand of sneakers or style of jeans, earrings, or hair styles that is popular this season. Young people should copycat the young people who still go to church rather than those who do drugs or engage in free sex. They should copycat other youth who set ambitious goals for their lives and take care of their bodies rather than copycat the peers who make no plans for the future, abuse their bodies and pollute their minds.

The Apostles chose to copycat Jesus' ministry of preaching and healing, to continue that valuable ministry that benefited so many. Many Christians abbreviate the title of the book The Acts of the Apostles to Acts. The full title reminds us of the Apostles' ministry of marvels and wonders, which copycatted the four Gospel accounts of Jesus' ministry. In this, we see plainly that Christ did not limit the power that He exercised. He wanted to share it and to see its use for good continue.

Jesus made it clear that power was not only reserved for the Apostolic Age, but was given for all time. Clearly,

Jesus was not only referring to the apostles when He said, "He who believes in me will also do the works that I do, and greater works than these will he do, because I go to the Father" (John 14:12).

The local church needs to be a powerhouse in the community, a powerhouse of faith and prayer, a powerhouse of love and caring. The Acts of the Apostles in the Bible is the story of a power that flowed from the day of Pentecost, when believers were full of the Holy Spirit, forward to the present time.

Notably, the Apostolic Church was not an economic or political powerhouse. It was not the intellectual powerhouse of the scholars. Indeed, it had no military power to force religion on anyone. The Apostolic Church didn't boast the power of numbers; it was a minority religion and would doubtless have been regarded as a questionable religious sect. Nevertheless, the power of God rested upon it, and was exercised in its midst, according to the account in Acts.

It is so easy to underestimate spiritual power and what it can do. Political, financial, military, and even personal power can appear so much more impressive to us at times. But, you can put spiritual power up against all the other powers of the world and it will win. Remarkably, the spiritual power of the Christian believers outlasted all the grandeur and power of the Roman Empire. And the Church of Jesus Christ marches and prays on, while kings and dictators rise and fall. Think of a few spiritual giants over the years and how they helped to change the world. Their names fill many books and adorn the Book of Life in heaven.

James, in his New Testament letter to "the twelve tribes scattered among the nations," encouraged Christians to pray that the sick would be made well with these words:

> Is any among you sick? Let him call for the elders of the
> church, and let them pray over him, anointing him with
> oil in the name of the Lord; and the prayer of faith will
> save the sick man, and the Lord will raise him up; and if
> he has committed sins, he will be forgiven.
>
> —James 5:14, 15

James was encouraging Christian believers to make use of the faith and prayer power available to all followers of Jesus. For indeed, God's people *do* have power and they should not be too timid to exercise it—especially if others can benefit from its use.

Remember, there are other powers in the world trying to tear down the efforts of spiritual power: evil powers of darkness orchestrated by Satan. There could be a book written called *The Acts of the Demons.* That book would record all the awful deeds of demon-possessed people over the centuries who have destroyed and killed mercilessly. With the body of evidence for evil that surrounds us, anyone who doesn't believe in the demonic is simply not awake today!

The Acts of the Demons would record the activity of the spirit of hatred that has given rise to wars and crimes, bigotry and racism, terrorism and abuse, violence and murder. *The Acts of the Demons* would reveal the roots of corruption, lying, cheating, and deceit. It would document the waste and extravagances of greed and oppression and tell how sexual perversion and immorality were inspired and promoted. *The Acts of the Demons* would brag about the arson, bombs, land mines, drunkenness, drug abuse, and genocide by dictators (like Adolph Hitler) that demons brought into the world to spoil God's creation.

When I went to the Holocaust Museum in Washington D.C., I was appalled to see how evil and cruel people can become when controlled by the demonic in the quest for world power and a super race. This demonic power in the world must be what Paul was referring to in his letter to the Christian Church at Ephesus in modern day Turkey:

> For we are not contending against flesh and blood, but against the principalities, against the powers, against the world rulers of this present darkness, against the spiritual hosts of wickedness in the heavenly places.
> —Ephesians 6:12

People have been lied to by rulers and leaders who have done everything they could to destroy religious beliefs. Under Communism, atheism became the state ideology and was forced on an entire population. But in the shadow of Karl Marx, Lenin, and Stalin, Christian believers continued to use spiritual power even when their church buildings were confiscated and their leaders killed, leaving them with only their faith and prayers.

Throughout history, the Church has survived one persecution after another. Christ's power is stronger than all the powers of the world. Indeed, Christ wants His followers to continue to use the power He offers for good in today's dark world. He offers His own authority to God's people, to be exercised as He modeled it on earth. Power to the people! Power to God's people today!

> And He called the twelve together and gave them power and authority over all demons and to cure diseases, and He sent them out to preach the Kingdom of God and to heal.
> —Luke 9:1, 2

Chapter Summaries and Study Guide

SEE HOW JESUS USED POWER!

Chapter One: "HE COULD CALM A STORM." Jesus used His power to calm a storm that threatened His disciples in a fishing boat. His words commanded the wind to be still. Then He calmed the fears of His disciples. That is power! To witness someone stilling a storm would be awesome. Peter tried to tap into such power and for a moment walked on water, but fear overcame him and he began to sink. *Fear was the enemy, not the storm. Not the wind, not the waves, but lack of faith was the problem. In what area of your life could overcoming fear cause you to walk in greater faith towards God?*

Chapter Two: "A BOY'S LUNCH FEEDS THOUSANDS." Can a few people with few resources be part of something great—all because our Lord can still multiply those resources many times over? If so, modern Christians need to dream of what, with God's help, *can be*, and to seek a new vision of the greater capability of local churches and of individual believers to embrace their limitless potential rather than obstacles.

Jesus used a boy's lunch and His twelve disciples to accomplish the distribution of necessary food to the multitudes, making them willing *participants* in the miracle rather than just spectators. Problems in the modern world loom so large that people don't know where to begin to solve them. Jesus cared about people. He wanted His disciples to care, too. That is where to start! Jesus started with *love*. Power in the hands of loving and caring people can do a lot for needy people and make a big difference. *How could you use the power God has placed in your hands more fully to accomplish His will?*

Chapter Three: "TEAM MINISTRY FAITH." The miracle of the restored paralytic man is not only a celebration of awesome power and healing, but is also a celebration of the faith of four men who had the daring to bypass any obstacle for the sake of a friend . . . because they had the faith to believe that Jesus could do anything. *Team ministry* thinks of people who can't get around well. Team ministry must also think of people who may look all right, but are emotionally crippled—people who may be suffering great emotional pain. It took *four* men in a team ministry working *together* to get their friend to the front row before Jesus. One Good Samaritan, even with a good heart, couldn't have done what those four men did. When Christians pray for the sick, they need to remember to include not only the physically sick, but also the emotionally, mentally, and spiritually sick within their community and their world. *Are you called to take part in some Team Ministry?*

Chapter Four: "DO WHAT HE SAYS." The blind man did not try to tell Jesus what to do. Jesus told him. Jesus did not use power to force the blind man to go and wash in the Pool of Siloam. Jesus withheld His power until the blind man followed His directions. Jesus expected people to do what He said to do. He never forced His way on people. He expected His directions to be followed as a *personal choice* and an individual decision. Yet, despite His clear directions, the world still sits in darkness. Things could be better if Jesus were taken more seriously today and if the world's people would decide to do what He said. *Is there something Jesus has made clear that He wants you to do?*

Chapter Five: "AN AMPUTATED EAR RESTORED" Jesus was trying to rectify a wound inflicted by one of His closest disciples. When His own life was at stake, He cared about someone else's ear. As is too often the case, Jesus had to undo what a misguided disciple had done. Where did religious people ever get the idea that they should try to advance the Christian faith with violence? Church history records countless tortures and murders that were perpetrated to "defend" the true faith against unbelievers and heretics by the sword through the union of Church and State. When Jesus told Peter to put the sword away to defend Him, many of Christ's followers over the centuries didn't understand what He said.

People of different religions have, for centuries, been known to justify killing for the sake of their religion in order to *force* particular beliefs on people. Jesus did not come to steal life away but to bring life. He never advocated death for non-believers, but endeavored to change people from within and to convert them by love rather than by the sword.

Misguided zeal on behalf of strong religious beliefs and conviction can do and has done terrible things. Such zeal ordered the crucifixion of the Savior. Sadly, such zeal practiced by Church leaders initiated the deaths of many of

See How Jesus Used Power!

Christ's followers and of countless non-Christians throughout Church history, setting a bad example to follow. *How
can your zeal for the Gospel of the Lord better reflect the wise
and loving character of Jesus?*

Chapter Six: "THE FAITH TOUCH" In other healing miracles
performed by Jesus, people came begging to Him for help—
or Jesus himself noticed people who needed help. This story
is different. Jesus never even saw the "woman with an issue
of blood." She never asked for help. Hers was a *silent* cry
for relief. Not a word was said, yet she was made well in an
instant. The crowd never noticed what happened. But Jesus
noticed instantly that something had happened. He sensed
that some of His reserve power had been drained off by
someone.

This woman, who pressed through the crowd to touch
the hem of Jesus' garment, might have been drained of financial resources, but she was not drained of faith resources!
If you want to get to Jesus badly enough, you'll work around
all the obstacles that get in the way and reach out and touch
Him. No crowd could stop her. She sensed the power that
Jesus had, and believed that if she could but touch something He was wearing, she would be healed. She never
thought she would be noticed. She might have said to herself, "Who am I? I'm a nobody. What right do I have to go
up to Jesus and ask Him for something?" Nevertheless, Jesus
did not rebuke her; He healed her. *What do you desperately
need from Jesus today, and how persistently will you seek it of
Him?*

Chapter Seven: "IF YOU DON'T WANT TO KNOW, DON'T ASK."
Great things have been accomplished in life because some
have dared to believe something could be done, while others doubted. Great insight has come to some who have dared

to ask for an honest answer to why they were unable to attain their goals or to move some "mountain." Jesus' reminder to His disciples of their lack of faith was like a call to arms. Jesus was not an information center. He gave *directives*, not advice. He gave commands and mandates, not suggestions. The Church must never settle for doling out religious information. The Church exists to put people in touch with Jesus Christ, God's powerful Son, and to prepare people to hear Jesus' directives and to experience His power. *Do you really want an answer to the question you are asking God today?*

Chapter Eight: "CAN A DEAD MAN FOLLOW ORDERS?" In three stories in the Gospels where Jesus' miraculous raising of dead persons is recorded, He spoke to each of them and gave the order to rise up. How powerful the *spoken* word of Jesus was! The *voice* of the Master raised the dead. Jesus Christ has the power to raise sinners from *death of the soul* for this life and for all eternity. *Has he resurrected your spirit and called you to walk in "newness of life" today?*

Chapter Nine: "RELEASED FROM MADNESS" The former homeless madman would no longer wander naked and aimless among the graves of the dead. He had found new life in Christ! The chains of demonic possession and spiritual bondage were broken when Christ spoke. He was now living evidence of Christ's miraculous power. The hope now for that community would be *one* restored man who could tell how Jesus had released him from his mental illness and demonic possession.

The man would now be an evangelist for Jesus, just like the other disciples. Even as Jesus was no longer welcome in that community, in spite of the good He had done with His spiritual power, so Jesus would not be welcome today in every community, boardroom, or government gathering. He would not be welcome in every synagogue, mosque, temple, or even in every church. The Bible talks very frankly about demons and demon possession. How else can one explain so many crazed acts of violence in the modern world today? *Where Jesus is not welcome, what other forces of darkness move in and take up cruel dominion?*

Chapter Ten: "NOW THAT HE HAS TOUCHED A LEPER..." After Jesus had touched the leper, would *you* have wanted to be the next person He would touch? Jesus told the restored man not to tell anyone how the miracle had happened. Jesus told the man to go to the priest first and to go through the prescribed cleansing ritual. Then he would have the necessary *proof* that indeed he was well again. Then people would believe the miracle.

But no, the man didn't listen. He hadn't gone through the process outlined in the Mosaic Law, so nobody believed in his healing. *Premature* religious talk can turn people away rather than convince others. Many don't want to hear the testimony of some persons, because their words are not backed up by their lives. The reason Jesus used His God-given power to heal people's bodies was because He cared about people. Because He *loved* people, He used His power to help them regain their lives and find *joy* again. Because He loved the total person, He would help them find salvation for their souls and minds as well as for their bodies. Healing of the body, then, was not Jesus *total* ministry; it was a vital part of His ministry. If Jesus had never healed anyone, it would only indicate that either He really didn't care enough about people and their hurts or else He lacked sufficient *power* to do anything miraculous. *Do people who know you find that your life matches your testimony?*

Chapter Eleven: "POWER TO GOD'S PEOPLE!" We hear so much about *copycat crimes.* Why are people so prone to copy evil and so little inclined to copy good behavior? Thank God for the apostles, who copied the *good* use of power by Jesus to care for people and to heal people's bodies. Jesus inspired His followers to *continue* what He started. Healing should not be just a fringe experience that happens at tent crusades, but should be *central* to all churches. We normally think of Jesus doing all the healing miracles in New Testament times. This is not so; Christ's disciples healed many people as they traveled, preaching the Gospel. It is often forgotten that Jesus *shared* His power with His disciples. He authorized them to go out and heal the sick, just as He was doing. *How can Christ use you to bring healing to this world?*

To order additional copies of

See HOW Jesus Used Power!

Have your credit card ready and call

Toll free: (877) 421-READ (7323)

or send $9.95** each plus $4.95 S&H* to

WinePress Publishing
PO Box 428
Enumclaw, WA 98022

www.winepresspub.com

**WA residents, add 8.4% sales tax

*add $1.00 S&H for each additional book ordered